W9-CFR-232

BANKER'S COMPLETE
LETTER BOOK

BANKER'S COMPLETE
LETTER BOOK

E. J. Harper

and

Donald L. Henry

PRENTICE-HALL, INC.   Englewood Cliffs, N.J.

Prentice-Hall International, Inc., *London*
Prentice-Hall of Australia, Pty. Ltd., *Sydney*
Prentice-Hall of Canada, Ltd., *Toronto*
Prentice-Hall of India Private Ltd., *New Delhi*
Prentice-Hall of Japan, Inc., *Tokyo*
Whitehall Books, Ltd., *Wellington, New Zealand*
Prentice-Hall of Southeast Asia Pte. Ltd., *Singapore*

© 1978 by

Prentice-Hall, Inc.
Englewood Cliffs, N.J.

Library of Congress Cataloging in Publication Data

Main entry under title:

Banker's complete letter book.

    Includes index.
    1. Banks and banking--Records and correspond-
ence. 2. Commercial correspondence. I. Harper,
E. J.   II. Henry, Donald L.
HG1616.R4B36   651.7'5'024332   78-4156
ISBN 0-13-055582-7

Printed in the United States of America

Dedication

To the loving memory of my daughter,
Mary Jane Harper Nelson.

—E. J. Harper

To my wife, Fay, with all my love.

—Donald L. Henry

About the Authors

E. J. Harper is a well known banking authority, currently serving as President and Chairman of the Board of a Missouri financial institution. As former President and Chairman of the Board of a Kansas bank as well, he brings on-the-job experience to the diverse requirements of present day fiduciary executives. A financial expert, he has conducted bank seminars for NCR Corporation attended by the major banks from every state. Mr. Harper has a wide acquaintanceship with members of the banking industry. He is a member of the Operations Committee of the Missouri Banker's Association and is active in the Independent Banker's Association as well as the American Banker's Association.

Donald L. Henry is a recognized credit authority and business executive and has received professional certification as a Certified Consumer Credit Executive. As an active business executive, writer, lecturer, and consultant he brings dynamic on-the-job solutions to the demanding communication requirements of the banking industry. Mr. Henry has gained wide executive experience in banking and credit card operations. He has held the post of Vice-President of Uni-Serv Corporation, a subsidiary of American Express, as well as at Chase Manhattan Bank. A graduate of Ohio State University, he has written numerous professional articles and is author of the book, *Henry on Credit and Collections*, Prentice-Hall, Inc.

What This Book
Will Do for You

This book compiles the best professional letters, memos and forms now used by America's foremost bankers. These proven letters gathered from over 100 banks are ready to use, or can be easily modified for your special requirements. You may well recognize some of the letters—impressive marketing letters are always talked about among bankers.

The tough letters to write have been done for you—by other bankers who have had to handle the same firing-line problems as you. Over 300 internal and external letters tested by the results obtained by bankers cover every possible need to write letters and memos; written in a style and tone that adds prestige and status to your communication skills. Even the bank collection letters have brought favorable comments from customers—*plus* the money.

What's your time worth? This book gives you problem-solved letters that will cut letter-writing . . . dictation . . . typing . . . proofreading . . . corrections . . . retyping—at least in half. For example, if you earn $30,000 then every minute is worth $.2561. If your secretary is paid $8,000 annually, that adds $.0726 for every minute of secretarial time on your letters. If you spend 20 minutes drafting a letter and the secretary spends 5 minutes on a special marketing letter; then your letter will cost $5.48 before postage.

Use this book for your special marketing letters to save time—aspirin—and possibly produce a superior message. Let the brainwork of other bankers go to work for you.

Each letter was carefully selected by bankers-for bankers, from among thousands of letters and memos now being used by banks. A coast-to-coast search in the letter files of over a hundred top banks produced the best letter for each function within banking. Some of the field-tested letters have been edited to provide more modern and more productive letters. These unique letters have been designed by actual bankers to cover the entire range of your banking requirements. All the letters you will ever need for the difficult assignments are included in this complete book.

NOTHING IS AS POWERFUL AS AN OUTSTANDING LETTER

Why do you need this book? What will it do for you? A few answers to these questions are given in the following checklist:

TWENTY-FIVE WAYS THIS BOOK WILL HELP YOU WRITE OUTSTANDING LETTERS AND MEMOS.

- Letters to encourage new deposits. For example, Letter B-21, that brought in a $110,000 deposit plus others. (See Group B)
- Need a new service? Try the Direct Deposit of Social Security Checks letter—letter B-27 resulted in 780 new savings accounts and 1,846 checking deposits. (See Group B)
- Letters to market installment loans that increase your share of the market. (See Group B)
- Sell the Debit Card and fingertip banking that customers need in the future EFTS Banking System. (See Group B)
- The better way to bank, Letter A-27, introducing Modular Money Management. (See Group A)
- New ways to request the financial statement from the customer who "forgets" to comply. (See Group E)
- The special problem letter—an apology for action of employee without offending either customer or employee. (See Group A)
- A unique purchasing letter declining to buy from a good bank customer without risking the loss of a corporate account. (See Group K)
- A results-oriented letter inviting use of a bank credit card,

that for one bank increased activation over 30 percent. (See Group B)

- The no-nonsense letter to tell a staff employee "no raise" this year, without losing staff dedication and loyalty. (See Group I)
- Special holiday greeting letters for customers which improve banking relationship with warmth. (See Group C)
- Innovative letters disclosing banking decisions that rally support and prevent dissatisfaction within the stockholder family. (See Group J)
- Letters using the psychologically proper responses to difficult community requests. (See Group H)
- Unique stockholder letters that motivate decision approval. (See Group J)
- Unique community-minded letters that compliment with either "Yes" or "No" answers. (See Group H)
- Responses to those tough Governmental Agency letters that reduce additional correspondence. (See Group L)
- A special bank memo that clearly defines authority of the chief executive for reduced operational delays and costs. (See Group N)
- Innovative letters that explain new and unique bank processing techniques without offending and losing established customers. (See Group A)
- The letter, "Buy Your Own Bank," that "sold" another banker on the purchase of a bank with better than average financial terms. (See Group M)
- Firing-line communications to help establish a bank merger or bank holding company. (See Group M)
- Trust and estate situation letters with powerful empathy that can promote increased Trust Department volume. (See Group D)
- Use the "How To Become a Millionaire" marketing letter that sparked the growth of one bank from 10.1 million dollars in assets to 14.9 million dollars in assets, within less than two years. (See Group B)
- The unique credit letter that averted a customer lawsuit and potential bank expense. (See Group E)
- Unique letters, such as Letter B-28, "Welcoming New Customers That Cross-Sell New Bank Services;" garner for your bank thousands of dollars of new business. (See Group B)

- Responses to difficult banking personal situations that reverse adverse situations to the bank's advantage. (See Group G)
- Plus hundreds of other outstanding problem-solving answers in ready-to-use letter form designed to reduce the cost of creating letters; and to carry a clearer, more distinct message to your reader for the best results.

HOW TO USE THIS BOOK

Now consider the additional important uses of this book:

- If you have a specific problem, for example, "How can I *sell* our bank customers on the Christmas Club Savings Plan and reduce the expense of operation to the bank?"; simply turn to the Locato-matic Letter Finder. This unique instant letter locater lists your major problems in communication followed by the letter code for the best letters that identify with your specific problem. Each letter has a group designate and a number code. A selected letter, such as A-22, will be quickly found in the Group A letters and numerically in the 22nd position.

  In the Locato-matic Letter Finder you will find "Christmas Club" followed by the reference A-22. Quickly turn to Group A, Forty-nine Customer Relations Letters That Win New Customers and Retain Old Ones. Turn to letter A-22, Christmas Club Letter That Retains Old Customers at Less Cost. Use this letter, or vary with paragraphs from other letters found in the book to convey your exact message. The chore of drafting successful letters is reduced to seconds by using the field-tested results of other bankers.

- If you are concerned about poor collection results, then turn to Group F, Thirty-seven Collection Letters. Select new or additional letters to add to your collection letter portfolio, from the top letters used from coast-to-coast. It is vital that collection letters be changed every few years for maximum results. Customer motivation to a collection letter is reduced when the same letter is received repeatedly. Use Group F letters to produce better collection results.

- Need special material for your stockholders? Then use Group J, Twenty-nine Innovative Stockholder Letters, and pick the brains of leading bankers who have the same requirements as you.

- Planning a new marketing approach for the bank? Want new business for your bank? Refer to Group B, Sixty-five Bank

Marketing Letters That Increase Profits and Volume. You will find eleven commercial banking letters, ten institutional letters, twenty-two retail banking letters, eight real estate marketing letters, and nine trust and investment marketing incentive letters. Implement these letters for specific bank functions—as they are; or modify the letters with paragraphs from other letters in the book, to give yourself an oustanding marketing program that can increase your share of the market—dramatically.

- Use this book as an outstanding reference to all the tough communications, such as: Employee Relations, Government Agencies, Community Activity, Bank Customer Relations and Internal Operations. You will find a letter that solves every major problem in communications.

- Use two books—one at your desk for creating powerful banking answers and one at your secretary's desk for perfect typing of better decision letters—a highly efficient way to conserve your valuable time.

Simply note your response decision on the letter to be answered. "A-22" marked on the incoming letter, for example, gives your secretary all the information required to type a powerful personal letter requiring your signature. Without interrupting your more valuable business activity, the secretary will use her book to locate letter "A-22" and complete your personalized letter. This unique method eliminates the expensive and time-consuming personal dictation. You can free yourself for the more productive and interesting challenges of the banking business with regular use of this book.

Start today by putting this book to work as a silent partner in better communications and reduce your personal workload.

Just ten of the over 300 field-tested letters in this book could save or earn for your bank thousands of dollars in six months.

E.J. Harper

Donald L. Henry

What's Your Letter Writing Time Worth?

Based on 244 eight-hour working days

You Earn	Every 15-Minutes Is Worth	Every Hour Is Worth	In a Year One Hour Per Day Is Worth
$ 8,000	$ 1.03	$ 4.10	$ 1,000
9,000	1.15	4.61	1.125
10,000	1.28	5.12	1,250
12,000	1.54	6.15	1,500
14,000	1.79	7.17	1,750
16,000	2.05	8.20	2,000
18,000	2.31	9.22	2,250
20,000	2.56	10.25	2,500
25,000	3.20	12.81	3,125
30,000	4.34	15.37	3,750
35,000	4.48	17.93	4,375
40,000	5.12	20.49	5,000
50,000	6.40	25.61	6,250
75,000	9.61	38.42	9,375
$100,000	$12.81	$51.23	$12,500

Locato-Matic Letter Finder

INSTANTLY LOCATE THE MODEL LETTER

To provide greater utility in selecting a letter for a given situation, this instant letter locater is provided for quick cross reference for major banking communication subjects. It serves as an adjunct to the Subject Index which appears at the end of the book. Use the Locato-Matic Letter Finder for rapid location of the major banking subjects. The letter code will identify the type of message contained in each letter. Greater versatility is at your fingertips to select the best letter to suit your exact requirement, or select partial paragraphs from several letters listed under the same heading.

For quick notation of the letter contents, the letter codes are as follows:

A—Customer Relations in Banking
B—Bank Marketing Letters
C—Goodwill Letters
D—Trust and Estate Situations
E—Credit Requirement Situations
F—Bank Collection Letters
G—Personal Situations
H—Community Activity
I —Bank Employee Relations

J —Bank Stockholder Letters
K—Purchasing Problems
L—Government Agency Responses
M—Special Banking Situations
N—Bank Operations Memos—Internal

AUTOMATIC TELLER MACHINES (ATM)

B-29, B-31, B-32

BANK CREDIT CARD LETTERS

A-29, A-32, A-33
B-3, B-4, B-7, B-18, B-24, B-33, B-34, B-35
E-2, E-5, E-7, E-14, E-16, E-19, E-23
F-3, J-5, N-2

BRANCH BANKING

A-29, A-43
B-13, B-14, B-16, B-17, B-25, B-31, B-36, B-37
C-5, C-12
I-14, J-17

CHARITY DONATIONS

G-4, H-2, H-4, H-5, H-6, H-10, H-14

CHECK ENDORSEMENTS

E-12, E-13

CHECKING ACCOUNT PROGRAMS

A-12, A-16, A-18, A-25, A-26, A-27, A-28
B-2, B-6, B-15, B-22, B-24, B-25, B-26, B-27, B-28, B-29, B-30, B-32, B-39, B-45, B-54
J-10, L-4, N-2

CHRISTMAS CLUB

A-22

COLLECTION LETTERS

F-1 to F-37, G-3

COMBINED STATEMENT

A-23, A-34, B-32

COMMERCIAL LOAN PROGRAMS

B-2, B-6, B-7, B-9, B-10, B-11, B-13, B-15, B-19, B-47, B-50
E-9, E-33, E-33, E-34, E-37
G-5, G-13, G-15
L-3

COMMUNITY ACTIVITY SITUATIONS

H-1 to H-15

COMPUTER PROCESSING

A-23, A-26, A-34, A-48
B-34, B-59
D-11, E-22, J-15

CREDIT EXTENSION LETTERS

E-1 to E-37

DEATH SITUATIONS

D-1, D-4, D-19
G-20, G-21, G-25
H-14, I-12

DEBIT CARDS—BANKING

B-29, B-31, B-32

DIRECT DEPOSIT PROGRAMS

A-16
B-26, B-27, B-29
G-16
L-5, L-6

EMPLOYEE RELATIONS—BANKING

I-1 to I-17
N-3, N-4, N-7, N-8

Acknowledgments

The authors express their thanks and gratitude to the individuals represented by the following 117 organizations for their interest and contribution of letters of better banking communications; or of the forward-thinking banking concepts that are reflected in this book:

American Bankers Association
American Bank of Maryland
The American Bank of Central Ohio
American National Bank & Trust
American National Bank of Omaha
American National Bank of Parma
American State Bank of Oswego
Atlantic National Bank
Bank of America N.T. & S.A.
Bank of the Commonwealth
Bank of Dwight
Bank of Kincaid, Kansas
The Bank of New York
Bank of Olympia
Bank of Pahokee
Bankers Trust Company
Board of Governors of Federal Reserve System
B.M.C. Durfee Trust
Brenton Bank of Des Moines
Bucklin State Bank of Bucklin, Missouri
Bushton State Bank
Cabarrus Bank & Trust Company
Capital Bank & Trust of Belton
Chase Manhattan Bank N.A.
Chemical Bank of New York
Citibank N.A.
Citizens and Southern National Bank

Citizens Bank of Blount County, Tennessee
Citizens National Bank
Citizens National Bank & Trust Company of Columbus, Ohio
Cleveland Trust Company
Commerce Bank of Kansas City N.A.
Continental Bank
Continental Illinois National Bank & Trust Company
Crocker National Bank
Dai-Ichi Kangyu Bank
Detroit Bank & Trust Company
Euclid National Bank of Cleveland
Exchange National Bank
Farmers Bank of Polo
Federal Reserve Bank of Kansas City
Fidelity Bank N.A.
First Bank & Trust of Boynton Beach, Florida
First City National Bank of Houston
First Knox National Bank of Mt. Vernon, Ohio
First Midwest Bancorp, Inc.
First National Bank & Trust Company of Tulsa
First National Bank of Carbondale
First National Bank of Chicago
First National Bank of Cincinnati

First National Bank of Dallas
First National Bank of Dayton
First National Bank of Denver
First National Bank of Kansas City
First National Bank of Midland
First National Bank of Orlando
First National Bank of St. Charles
First National Bank of St. Louis
First National Bank of St. Joseph, Missouri
First National Bank of Springfield
First National Bank of Wynne, Arkansas
First Pennsylvania Bank
First State Bank of Columbus
First State Bank of Thayer
The Franklin Bank
The German American Bank of Jasper, Indiana
The Gettysburg National Bank
Guaranty Bank & Trust Company
Harris Trust & Savings Bank
Huntington National Bank of Columbus
Irving Trust Company
Lagonda National Bank of Springfield
Lasalle National Bank
Manufacturers Hanover Trust Company
Manufacturers National Bank of Detroit
Mars National Bank
Mellon Bank N.A.
Mercantile Bank
Michigan Bank N.A.
Michigan National Bank of Lansing
Mid-America Automated Clearing House Association
Missouri Bankers Association
Monroe Banking & Trust Company of Aberdeen, Mississippi
Morgan Guaranty
National Bank of Detroit

National Bank of North America N.A.
North Country Bank
Northern Trust Bank
Northwest Bank & Trust Co. of Davenport, Iowa
Northwest National Bank of Chicago
Ohio National Bank
Ohio State Bank
Piedmont Bank & Trust Bank
Pittsburgh National Bank
The Planers National Bank of Rocky Mount, North Carolina
Reeves Bank
Republic National Bank of Dallas
Second National Bank of Richmond
Security National Bank of Springfield
Security Pacific National Bank
Southeast First National Bank of Miami
Southeast National of Concordville, Pennsylvania
Southshore National Bank
Sumitomo Bank, Ltd.
Tarheel Bank & Trust of Gatesville, North Carolina
Texas National Bank of Commerce in Houston
Third National Bank of Dayton
Traders National Bank of Kansas City
Union National Bank of Manhattan, Kansas
United Bank of Denver
United California Bank
United Missouri Bank of Kansas City N.A.
Valley National Bank of Phoenix
Wachovia Bank & Trust Company
Wells Fargo Bank
Winters National Bank & Trust Company
The Yardville National Bank

And also:

Fay Henry, Belinda Henry, and Gregory Henry for their creative talents in making the material more meaningful and useful to bankers everywhere, and a special thanks to Gary Henry.

GROUP *A* LETTERS

Forty-nine Banking Customer Relations Letters That Win New Customers and Retain Old Ones

- 11 winning commercial customer relations letters
- 10 institutional customer relations letters
- 12 convincing retail banking customer letters
- 10 motivating real estate letters
- 6 trust and investment customer relations letters

Customer relations is really the heart of banking. Maintaining the continued patronage of present customers and expecting new customers to know about the special banker-customer loyalty, is only done with an organized program. The Group A letters offer forty-nine banking customer relations letters that win new customers and retain old ones as part of that plan.

Banking customers receive impressions of banks based on many factors—positive and negative—some you can control, and some are beyond your control. From our surveys, we have found that the larger the banking staff the more important it became to concentrate on building positive customer relations attitude. To help build and maintain this positive attitude, the forward-thinking banker replies to all customer inquiries promptly (within two days), and with friendly and helpful responses. Delays in responding will create negative impressions from your customers. Therefore, it is important to respond quickly. If you know there will be a delay, send an acknowledgment that tells when a complete answer will be sent.

The letters in this group provide tailor-made responses that allow you to respond immediately to customer relations requirements. These letters are prepared to gain positive reception to continued banking service from the best people in the world—your customers.

SPECIAL THANK YOU TO OLD CORPORATE ACCOUNTS LETTER

LETTER A-1

Regularly timed messages to customers generate loyalty and continued patronage.

Dear _____:

Have you ever met an old friend at a business meeting—one you hadn't seen for years but occasionally think about? It's a great thrill!

That has just happened to me. While reviewing the bank business accounts that I have personally opened, I noticed your name. I was able to recall when you first opened your corporate account on _____, 19____. Yes, I remember your telling me about your plans for the company. Your present success is written on your business account and reads like a history book.

We've grown, too. Hopefully, we have offered the services like an old friend should. As your business continues to expand, remember your friends at ABC Bank are here to be of service.

Very truly yours,

FINANCIAL STATEMENTS FOR
SPECIAL BANKING SERVICES LETTER

LETTER A-2

A customer relations letter stressing the benefits of supplying that required financial statement—now.

Dear Customer:

To be of better service to you, it is necessary for us to request a copy of your financial statement for the end of your business year.

This information, supplied in confidence, enables your bank to furnish loan services. Also, new bank services for your company can be recommended based on the needs dictated by your financial statement.

With your statement on hand, we can be useful as a bank reference. If you wish for us to be your bank reference, please tell us—allowing us to disclose information concerning our banking relationship.

Please send your financial statement to me as soon as possible. Should you want any assistance in preparing the statement, call me.

Cordially,

THE CLOSED ACCOUNT LETTER

LETTER A-3

Whenever a commercial account closed out a banking relationship, one bank found this letter improved customer relations. Several important accounts were reactivated.

Dear _____:

Our records do not indicate the reason you closed your checking account with the ABC Bank.

Because of the importance of your banking program to us, would you please take a minute to tell me why you made this decision?

( )   1. Either the bank or an employee didn't give the quality of service you expect. Please tell me where we failed so we can improve our service.

( )   2. The account is no longer needed. Please tell me what has happened to change your requirements.

( )   3. A reason we haven't mentioned. Please tell us why.

I would appreciate hearing from you, along with any additional comments you would care to make. Please use the enclosed envelope for your reply.

Sincerely,

President

"INSUFFICIENT FUNDS"—CORPORATE ERROR LETTER

LETTER A-4

Good customer relations require softening the errors of valued customers.

Dear Mr. ＿＿＿＿:

I don't blame you for being upset about the error in returning your corporate check back to the XYZ Company as "insufficient funds."

Apparently, the XYZ Company presented the check written for a substantial amount prior to the date typed on the check. It is unwise to issue any check prior to the date you want it presented for payment. I'm just sorry our teller, who normally watches the date of issue, did not refuse to accept for deposit the check in question.

However, I will send the attached letter of explanation to the XYZ Company to clarify your long business relationship with the ABC Bank.

With warmest personal regards,

GETTING THE "INSUFFICIENT FUNDS" CUSTOMER OUT OF "HOT WATER"

LETTER A-5

Helping your banking customer out of a bad situation will create long-term goodwill. This letter is the companion to Letter A-4.

Dear XYZ Company:

Please accept our apology for any inconvenience caused by the return of your check from the DEF Company as "insufficient funds."

We at the ABC Bank wish to assure you that sufficient funds were on deposit on the date the check was intended to be presented for payment. Apparently, your company did not notice the future date on the DEF check. Of course, we frown on checks being written with a future date. It will occasionally create just the problem that happened at our bank.

Unfortunately, our teller did not notice the date either. Normally, we would not accept the check for deposit because of the future date for posting the check. On behalf of the DEF Company, which has an excellent record with the bank, we hope the errors did not cause you any inconvenience.

With warmest personal regards,

SEARCHING FOR THE CUSTOMER'S PREVIOUS CORRESPONDENCE LETTER

LETTER A-6

How to say, "Send another copy of your correspondence," with grace.

Dear ———:

We've searched everywhere in the bank . . .

Yet we have not been able to locate your previous correspondence. This is most unusual for us, as it is rare to have any of our mail go astray.

We are eager to assist you, and must request your help. Would you provide us with a copy of your previous letter? Upon receipt of this material, you can be assured your banking question will be given our immediate attention.

Thank you for your cooperation and patience.

Cordially,

INTRODUCING A VALUED COMMERCIAL CUSTOMER LETTER

LETTER A-7

A local business making a special presentation in another part of the country will need references and a portfolio of introduction. The bank is one of the best references for good customers.

To Whom It May Concern:

By way of this letter, the ABC Bank is pleased to introduce the XYZ Company, 111 Any Street, Newtown, Ohio.

The XYZ Company is well respected in our community and has maintained an excellent banking relationship for the past seven years with ABC Bank. Because of our close advisory capacity, we are able to state that the company is financially stable. We of course do not hesitate to provide financial assistance when the XYZ Company requests our commercial banking services. You will find the XYZ Company favorably listed by the respective trade rating services.

Any courtesy you show the XYZ Company will be greatly appreciated.

Cordially,

CREATING AGREEMENT CUSTOMER RELATIONS LETTER

LETTER A-8

Getting commercial banking customers to agree with you is a skill that takes practice to acquire. This ability is a prime requirement for banking success. This letter creates agreement and retains old customers.

Dear _____:

We appreciate your banking patronage. All of our services are intended to make banking easier and more efficient for you.

However, it is our aim to improve banking for your benefit. That is why we were interested in your letter comment, "We tried something like this before and it didn't work." Your situation is probably different, but do you feel that what you tried in the past won't work now?

Please let us know what there is about the payroll to employee checking account transfer plan that is causing you concern. Once in operation, how much time do you think it would save each month? We will be happy to coordinate the various facets with your company, in order to modify the plan for a more efficient processing and banking benefit to your company.

We will look forward to your response and the opportunity to correct the potential errors in your past experience. Together, we can create a program advantageous to your company and to your employees.

Cordially,

WELCOME TO A NEW BUSINESS ENTERPRISE LETTER

LETTER A-9

Letters of welcome to new businesses are valuable customer relations contacts.

Dear _____:

Welcome!

We just read the announcement of your new business in the business section of the newspaper. Launching a new enterprise is a rewarding and exciting undertaking. Since you have chosen us for your banking needs, we are delighted to be of service whenever the occasion arises.

You have our best wishes for a successful business future.

Cordially,

CONGRATULATIONS TO AN EXPANDING BUSINESS LETTER

LETTER A-10

Customer relations will be enhanced by congratulating the expansion of a bank customer.

Dear _____:

Congratulations on the opening of your new branch location.

It is always a pleasure to watch our bank customers expand their business. During the three years you have been banking with us, we have noticed your successful business plans.

The additional location will bring new challenges, and we want to let you know that the ABC Bank is your friend in banking.

Sincerely,

CONGRATULATIONS TO A PROMOTED BUSINESS EXECUTIVE

LETTER A-11

This letter congratulates the promoted executive with the opening of a new business location.

Dear Mr. _____:

We were delighted to read the announcement that the ZXR Company will open a new location at _____. with you named as the new manager. You have our congratulations on your new position.

Your new position will include added responsibilities which we know you can handle with skill. If your new duties require banking services, please contact Mr. _____, manager of ABC's branch near your new location.

Best wishes for your future success.

Cordially,

GETTING THE NEW CUSTOMER INTRODUCED
TO BANKING LETTER

LETTER A-12

In stressing a point-of-difference, a bank can win new customers and retain old ones.

Dear Mr. _____:

Your name was on the special list of new bank customers who have opened checking accounts within the past month. I personally review this list to determine if our other banking services can be of benefit to you. Perhaps, you may have an interest in our Savings Account program. It is our desire to offer services that will be convenient and profitable.

While in the bank transacting other business, it would only take a few minutes to activate a savings program. We offer automatic transfers from the checking account to the savings account in accordance with your authorization. These transfer deposits need not be large, but if regularly continued, will soon amount to a sizable amount.

The staff of your bank is constantly working to make and hold friends, and will do everything necessary to earn your respect. We want to make banking at ABC Bank more profitable for you. It is our pleasure to count you as a customer and friend.

Cordially,

BEST DEAL IN TOWN SAVINGS LETTER

LETTER A-13

Let the customer be aware that you are years ahead of competition.

Dear Customer:

For the past three years, ABC Bank has been doing what some other banks are just starting to do—giving you the best possible rate of return on your Savings Account by compounding your ___% interest continuously; 24 hours a day, 365 days a year.

It's proof that ABC Bank always tries to do more for your money—not just when competition forces it.

There's always a good reason to open a ___% Silver Savings Account at ABC Bank. The minimum balance you're required to keep in the ____% Silver Savings Account for at least 90 days is $250—not the $500 or $1000 that many other banks demand.

Good News from

ABC Bank

"OUR BUSINESS IS SERVICE" LETTER

LETTER A-14

An excellent institutional customer relations letter that stresses bank service.

Dear Customer:

We appreciate your business.

From all 21 of our staff members at ABC Bank we want to tell you that our business is service. Even though banking is money to some people, it is more than that to a moderate size bank like ABC Bank. We believe that service to our over 3,000 checking account customers and over 5,000 passbook savings account customers is our most important benefit.

We, at ABC Bank, try to see things from your point of view. That's why we try to continuously improve our services and provide the kind of banking you want.

Stop by and chat with us, anytime. You are always welcome at the ABC Bank.

Sincerely,

MORE REASONS TO BANK WITH US LETTER

LETTER A-15

A unique customer relations letter for existing customers, designed to pique their curiosity and implant the idea of more services.

Dear Customer:

We just counted up the many ways we can help you in banking services. Even *we* did not realize that we now offer you *THIRTY-EIGHT* reasons for the best financial package in town.

Ask the teller, the next time you are in the ABC Bank for the full list. You will be surprised, too!

Here's just a sample of a few of the thirty-eight services:

- Free notary service
- Free downtown parking (one hour)
- Free personalized memo sheets
- Automatic savings from checking
- Free telephone transfer of funds
- ___% interest on one-year Certificates of Deposit
- and thirty-two other super services

Thank you for banking ABC . . . and be sure you are using all of the services available.

Cordially,

BETTER BANKING WITH SAVINGS TRANSFER LETTER

LETTER A-16

The benefits of automatic checking account transfers are stressed.

Dear Customer:

You can still fill out a deposit slip—write a check to your savings, send it in the mail or drive to the bank. But why bother?

There is an easier and less expensive way to save. Simply decide how much you want to save each month. Ask the bank teller for automatic checking-to-savings transfer. Your savings are automatically transferred each month on the same day you choose—as little as $5. You save time, effort and expense. We help do your saving for you—automatically.

Stop at any branch office teller's window for an easier way to save money.

Cordially,

ABC Bank

"HAVE A FREE LUNCH ON US" LETTER

LETTER A-17

An innovative customer relations letter, that sparked considerable discussion and a transfer of a quarter of a million dollars in savings accounts from other banks.

Dear Customer:

Your savings account just got a break from ABC Bank.

We pay the highest interest rate banks currently can pay by law—5%. But *now*, we compound interest daily. Previously, we compounded interest quarterly. That is great news for you!

How? It means the price of a free lunch for your birthday from ABC Bank.

It works this way, $10,000 compounded quarterly at 5% earned $509.40, annually. But, $10,000 compounded daily at 5% earns $512.60 for a full year. The difference of $3.20 is extra earnings for each $10,000 on deposit for a full year. Not a lot of money, but the price of a reasonable lunch for your birthday.

The second $10,000 will let you invite your spouse for lunch, too. Your bank is finding ways to bring you more living from your savings account.

See you at lunch!

Cordially,

ABC Bank

MISSING PAYMENT ON INSTALLMENT LOAN LETTER

LETTER A-18

A request for a copy of a cancelled check, or a new check to replace the "lost" payment.

Dear _____:

We are sorry that we are unable to locate the payment for your installment loan.

We would like your assistance in tracing the missing payment. Would you furnish us with a copy of both sides of the cancelled check in your possession? You may bring it to the closest branch, if convenient. The ABC Bank teller can make a copy or notify us of the identification code we need to correctly credit your loan.

If the check in question has not been cancelled, you should stop payment and issue a replacement.

Your cooperation is greatly appreciated.

Cordially,

APOLOGY FOR DEPOSIT CREDITED IN ERROR LETTER

LETTER A-19

When the rare event happens—a checking account deposit incorrectly credited to the wrong customer—the customer benefited must be notified.

> Dear _____:
>
> We apologize . . .
> for the error on your checking account statement.
>
> You were erroneously given credit for a deposit of $_____
> on the date _____. The bank has applied the deposit to
> the proper customer and this amount will be corrected on your
> checking account as of this date.
>
> We regret any inconvenience caused and thank you for banking with the ABC Bank.
>
> Cordially,

NEW FREE SERVICE FOR SAVERS ONLY LETTER

LETTER A-20

Cement customer relations with announcement of new services for existing customers.

> Dear Bank Saver:
>
> The ABC Bank offers a new service just for existing customers.
> Every savings account owner is now entitled to one free money
> order or cashier's check, each and every month.
>
> Whenever you need a money order or cashiers check, for any
> amount, you are entitled to the first one each month—free!
>
> This is just one of our ways of saying "THANK YOU" for saving
> at ABC Bank. Don't forget, if you have any banking requirements, be sure to ask us. You may be glad you did!
>
> Cordially,

THE INACTIVE CHECKING AND SAVINGS ACCOUNT LETTER

LETTER A-21

A letter designed to activate the inactive checking and savings customer. This letter was successful in airing several complaints, while increasing checking and savings activity.

Dear Customer:

The ABC Bank would like to renew a pleasant and old acquaintance.

A review of your savings and checking account, indicate both have been inactive during the past six months. If that is your wish, it is fine with us. But if for some reason you have found our service less than friendly or less than you desire, we would like to know about it.

It is our firmest desire to be of service to each and every banking customer. We want you to have the opportunity to enjoy the best in banking. Free notary service, use of a bank credit card, low cost installment loan service and free checking account benefits are just a few of the banking services we do offer you.

It's simple, we just want to be YOUR banker. If we can be of service in banking, please call upon us. We are as close as your nearest branch.

Cordially,

CHRISTMAS CLUB LETTER THAT RETAINS OLD CUSTOMERS AT LESS COST

LETTER A-22

The bank utilizing this letter improved customer relations with a 94 percent reactivation at an 18 percent cost reduction in processing. Activating the innovative automatic transfer technique for an old program—the Christmas Club Account—resulted in less paperwork and fewer manual handling transactions. Build customer relations in any required check mailing with creative communicator letters. Show empathy.

Dear Christmas Club User:

Christmas is almost here!

Your check for the balance in your _____ Bank Christmas Club is enclosed. We are pleased that you have used our Christmas Club service this year.

Your account will automatically remain open for next year's use. However, we would appreciate having you stop by the bank or telephone us at _____, to let us know what size check you desire for next year. Then we can send you a new coupon book.

Next year's club begins the week of November 15.

Last year we started a new automatic transfer program. If you took advantage of this, we will continue to debit your account in the same manner unless you notify us differently. Customers have told us this makes a savings program painless.

If you did not use the automatic transfer program, let me briefly explain its concept. On your request, we will transfer a specified amount to your Christmas Club Account automatically from your checking account. After the initial request, it requires no further action on your part. There are no checks to write—no coupons to mail. You need only deduct the amount from your checkbook each month; very similar to the method you use to subtract your service charges. Like service charges, these transfers show on your monthly statement.

If you have further questions or would like to take advantage of this new service, please call me at _____. We will be happy to help you. We sincerely appreciate having your account and wish to take this opportunity to wish you a very HAPPY HOLIDAY SEASON.

Cordially,

INTRODUCING THE COMPUTER BANK PROCESSING LETTER

LETTER A-23

A good customer relations letter introducing the "Combined" statement concept with customer service benefits.

Dear Bank Customer:

We would like to take this opportunity to introduce you to a new and unique method of bank processing made possible by our new computer.

Our unique method is called Central Information File. "CIF" is basically a method by which your varied associations with the _____ bank are grouped into one record for you. Before the advent of "CIF" this was not possible. But what does this mean to *you*, our customer? It means we are able to handle your various activities with us, faster and more efficiently than ever before. No longer are you a Savings Customer, a Checking Customer or Loan Customer. *You* are a personalized, important Bank Customer.

Now, as a bank customer you will receive a "Combined" Statement. All of your transactions with _____ Bank will be reported to you on *one* statement. With this month's statement we have improved the reporting of your Checking Account. Shortly thereafter, your statement will reflect the addition of other services as they become processed in a better form with your "Combined" statement.

Appearing on the reverse side of the statement are explanations for all symbols used on the statement; such as, "SC" for Service Charge.

If you have any questions regarding your new Combined Statement, please do not hesitate to contact our Customer Service Department. We appreciate serving you as an important Bank Customer.

Sincerely,

RETAIL BANKING POSTING ERROR APOLOGY LETTER

LETTER A-24

A field-tested advance letter to a good customer about to be billed for a credit charge; generally with a large dollar amount that previously was misfiled, posted in error to another customer's account, or unreadable in the original posting run. For large dollar amounts the advance letter is good customer relations that can prevent a complaint or delinquency.

Dear Customer:

Re: Bank Credit Card #_____

An audit of your account indicates that we failed to charge you for a purchase made several months ago at (name of merchant) in the amount of $_____. Therefore, this item will appear on your next statement.

We sincerely regret any inconvenience caused by the delay in properly posting this charge to your account.

We appreciate your shopping with (name of bank credit card).

Cordially,

SENIOR CITIZENS REMEMBERED FOR PLUS BUSINESS LETTER

LETTER A-25

Subject: "Dimension 60"

Dear Customer:

"Dimension 60" is an exclusive program of the ABC Bank for individuals 60-or-better.

It is a program of valuable services and benefits. To join, you must simply be 60-or-better and have (or open soon) a savings account at any ABC Bank. As a member, you're entitled to all benefits of "Dimension 60" . . . FREE.

Every valuable service is designed to make life more enjoyable for you . . . and a lot easier. Easier to handle your money and make it grow. Easier to make transactions. Easier to get things done. And in many cases, easier for you to get more for your hard-earned dollar.

"Dimension 60" members receive:

(1) FREE PHOTO IDENTIFICATION MEMBERSHIP CARD(S)

Your "Dimension 60" card signifies you're a member entitled to all the program benefits, and serves as permanent identification. Your name and social security number are printed on the color photograph card, then bonded in permanent sealed plastic.

(2) FREE CHECKING WITH FREE PERSONALIZED CHECKS

No minimum balance, monthly charge, service charge and no limit on the number of checks you write. Complete checking services *free*.

(3) FREE SEMINAR SERIES

A number of free seminars will be presented for the benefit of "Dimension 60" members. Among the more important topics to be covered:

- "How to protect your health after age 60"
- "How to avoid fraud and confidence schemes"
- "The in-and-outs of income tax preparation"
- "Choosing your investments"
- "Personal estate planning—it's for everyone"
- Updates on Medicare and Social Security benefits

(4) YOUR OWN PERSONAL BANKER

You'll receive individualized personal attention by your own Personal Banker who has the knowledge and authority to handle all your banking needs.

(5) FREE WILL AND TRUST COUNSELING

A qualified Trust Officer will review your present affairs and advise you on the need for a Will and other factors which may affect your present Will. Experience shows that almost everyone needs a Will. If you need Personal Estate Planning help, our Trust Officers will advise you on plans which could protect your assets, reduce estate taxes and probate costs, and suggest various plans to administer your affairs.

(6) FREE CASHIER'S CHECKS AND MONEY ORDERS

Whenever you need a cashier's check or money order, your "Dimension 60" membership makes them available at no service charge. Other benefits will be added from time to time.

(7) FREE INVESTMENT COUNSELING

We will be happy to suggest various ways to invest your money so that it will meet your requirements on safety and earn you the best possible return. We can offer you advice on bonds, stocks, Certificates of Deposit and other investment devices. We also have a full set of stocks and bonds record material available for you to inspect at no cost.

(8) FREE TRAVELER'S CHECKS

Traveler's checks in any denomination, for any total amount . . . no service charge.

(9) FREE GUARANTEED CHECK CARD

The card that's honored all over the St. Joseph/Savannah area for hassle-free acceptance of your personal checks for up to $100 cash or merchandise. Available to qualifying ABC Bank customers.

(10) SPECIAL DISCOUNT SAVINGS AT AREA BUSINESSES

Substantial savings for "Dimension 60" members! Your membership card will qualify you for discounts on prescriptions, meals and merchandise at participating pharmacies, restaurants and stores throughout the area.

(11) AUTOMATIC SOCIAL SECURITY OR BENEFIT CHECK DEPOSITS

(12) SPECIAL SOCIAL EVENTS AND LOW-COST GROUP TRAVEL

The whole "Dimension 60" group will be getting together for . . . money-saving national and international group travel arranged by professional travel agencies . . . custom weekend trips for lots of fun, close to home, at a low cost . . . special social gatherings to renew old acquaintances and make new friends.

(13) FREE "DIMENSION 60" NEWS BULLETINS

So you may keep up on all "Dimension 60" events, you will receive our "News Bulletin" from time to time. It will advise you of upcoming "Dimension 60" seminars, updated and new merchant discount information, travel plans, social security changes, tax hints and a host of other interesting and helpful information.

JOIN "DIMENSION 60" TODAY . . . FOR AN EASIER, MORE PLEASANT TOMORROW.

Cordially,

ANNOUNCING A CHANGE IN CHECKING SERVICE CHARGES LETTER

LETTER A-26

Any change in customer charges can create complaints. Stress a benefit to the customer in any change and then tell them. This letter informs of an INCREASE in service charges.

Dear Customer:

Your regular checking account will be changed to a *minimum* balance plan. Now, service charges will be applied to your checking account based on the *LOWEST ACTUAL* balance level as shown on your monthly statement.

Previously, you were charged on the *AVERAGE* balance level of your checking account. Now you can compute ahead and plan how to minimize your service charges.

The new schedule of service charges is:

If Your Minimum Balance During the Month Is	Charges Each Month Will Be:
$400 or above	-0-
300-399	$1
200-299	2
0-199	3

This improved method of computing service charges will take effect with the next checking account statement.

Now you are able to reduce or avoid service charges by planning your checking account balance each month. We urge you to keep your balance above $400 so that you may enjoy a checking account *without* paying a service charge.

We appreciate the opportunity to serve you with a simplified statement.

Sincerely,

MODULAR MONEY MANAGEMENT LETTER

LETTER A-27

An innovative letter that cross-sells other bank services that brought in several thousand dollars in new business from new and old customers.

Dear _____:

This letter introduces a better way to bank. We have entitled the program "MODULAR MONEY MANAGEMENT."

Modular Money Management is an entirely new and exciting way to fulfill your personal banking requirements. It is a combination of a large number of special benefits into one of the most attractive banking packages yet devised. The following is a list of some of the program's benefits:

ACTIVITY FREE CHECKING: Write as many checks as you wish without worrying about being charged per check. Only a 75¢ monthly maintenance charge is made, and is reduced by 10¢ for each $100 average balance you maintain. If your average exceeds $500, there is no maintenance charge.

REDUCED INSTALLMENT LOAN RATES: Upon qualifying for an installment loan, you receive a reduced rate. The savings can be substantial, especially upon the more expensive longer term items; such as automobiles and mobile homes.

SAVINGS INTEREST PAID FROM DATE OF DEPOSIT: Interest will be paid from date of deposit on your regular 5% per annum savings account, when deposits remain until the end of the quarter.

OVERDRAFT PROTECTION: Protection from returned checks can be yours through the ABC Bank. In addition, it permits you to actually write your own loans.

FREE, OPTIONAL FINANCIAL COUNSELING: At your disposal will be the entire expertise of the bank in the field of personal financial counseling. We will help you as much or as little as you wish, without charge and in complete confidence.

The ABC Bank is happy to welcome you to membership in the Modular Money Management Program. We invite you to take advantage of all the many financial services and benefits available through it. Since it has been specifically designed for you, your suggestions as to how we might improve it are enthusiastically encouraged.

Modular Money Management is a better way to bank and represents the results of the Bank's continuing efforts to give its customers the best in financial services.

Yours very truly,

A BETTER CHECKING ACCOUNT LETTER

LETTER A-28

Any change in procedure needs the customer benefit approach.

GOOD NEWS ABOUT YOUR CHECKING ACCOUNT!

We will begin adjusting the monthly charges on regular checking accounts with your next statement. The adjustment, according to the new monthly service charge schedule on the enclosed insert, is necessary in order to continue the same fine service; despite increasing costs.

Consolidated services—$2 a month.

The ABC Bank consolidated services account may represent a savings to you. Here is how: as a package of seven banking services that lets you write all the checks you want for just $2.00 a month—the lowest cost in town. In addition, you get free personalized checks, a 10% rebate on installment loan finance charges, automatic transfers to your savings account, overdraft checking loans, free traveler's checks, and 24-hour banking service.

Please let us know if you have any questions about the checking account price adjustment. If you would like to *see* how the consolidated services can save you money, just visit any branch office.

Thank you for banking ABC.

(*signed*)

INSTANT CASH BENEFIT LETTER

LETTER A-29

Stress the unique customer benefit of branch banking.

Dear _____:

You are never far from your money when you have an ABC Bank account. Just look at our area map!

We have more offices in the metropolitan area than any other bank. And you can use all of our offices interchangeably.

With your ABC checking or savings account, you can cash a check or make a savings transaction at the bank office nearest you—at home, at work or out shopping. We even have mini-offices in major supermarkets—just for you!

You can arrange for "instant cash" to spend at any office if you have your bank credit card.

It is simple, we just want to remain your bank.

ABC Bank

A CHANCE TO SAVE A LITTLE EXTRA MEANS MORE DOLLARS LETTER

LETTER A-30

A letter sent to existing savings account customers.

Results: 812 new savings accounts, 267 savings additions in excess of $1,000 each, plus others.

Dear Customer:

We have just posted your quarterly interest to your savings account at ABC Bank. As your banker, we are happy to be part of your savings plan.

Of course, the time to save is when you have the money in your hand:

- A bonus
- Dividend or interest checks
- An inheritance

But, if you are serious about the security of a savings plan, there is nothing like adding a little of each paycheck to your savings—BEFORE spending begins.

It is amazing how money GROWS . . . when you save regularly!

For example, $5 weekly savings will accumulate—at 5% a year—in 4 years to the amazing savings amount of *$1,475.62*. And in a short 10 years it will grow to *$3,367.42*, simply by saving only $5 weekly.

Think what that will buy in your future!

See any of our bank tellers to start your future savings security plan.

ABC BANK

BEING OUR CUSTOMER DOES MORE FOR YOU LETTER

LETTER A-31

Reasons why the customer should continue banking with the present bank.

Dear Customer:

If you have an ABC Bank Passbook Savings Account, you are one of the lucky ones.

While other banks have lowered the interest rates they pay on regular savings accounts, ABC Bank has held the line. You are not suddenly getting ½% less interest income for your hard-earned dollars. Even today, you are STILL earning a full ____% from day of deposit to day of withdrawal, compounded quarterly.

Why settle for less?

If you know someone who doesn't have a ____% ABC Bank regular passbook account, now is the time to give them a "hot" money tip—OPEN AN ABC BANK SAVINGS ACCOUNT! They can even have a savings account transferred from any other bank and we will take care of the transfer, too.

ABC BANK

"WE MISSED YOU" LETTER

LETTER A-32

Inactive Bank credit card customers can be reactivated at lower costs than soliciting new customers. This letter resulted in a reactivation of 12 percent of the mailing.

Dear Customer:

We missed you at ABC Bank.

When our customers want to use a bank credit card, we are pleased to have them available. However, our records indicate you have not used this service for quite some time. Of course if you no longer have use for a bank card, that is fine. We appreciate being able to extend the past service.

Your bank card is due to expire soon and your new card will be mailed to you, if you so desire. To insure that you receive the new bank card, please sign the enclosed request card and return it to us in the prepaid envelope.

We appreciate the opportunity to offer our many banking services to you.

Sincerely,

APOLOGY FOR LATE POSTING OF BANK CREDIT CARD PAYMENT LETTER

LETTER A-33

Payments sent close to the billing date of bank credit cards can create problems if the payment processing gets behind.

Dear _____:

Thank you for bringing to the bank's attention the error in assessing a finance charge on your bank credit card.

You are correct; we received your check on the closing date for the total balance due on the statement. Unfortunately, your check for $342.12 was posted on the following day, causing the finance charge of $5.13 to be added to your account. A credit for $5.13 will appear on your next statement to correct the error.

We are sorry for the mistake. We at ABC Bank hope you enjoy the convenience of shopping with the ABC credit card.

Cordially,

NEW FASTER REAL ESTATE PROCESSING LETTER

LETTER A-34

A customer relations letter that turns a customer change—possible inconvenience—into a customer benefit. Tell customers why that change was necessary—a new computer—and emphasize the customer benefits: new personalized coupon books and the new combined statement. A successful letter enabling the bank officer who created this marketing device, to introduce the new computer conversion and the changes required by the customer.

Dear Customer:

The improved processing of your real estate mortgage loan with the ABC Bank is the result of our new, faster computer.

The enclosed coupon book should be used for your regular monthly payment, as the loan payment book you have used in the past has been eliminated. You will notice that each coupon shows your name, real estate loan number and due date.

You can insure receiving proper credit by always using your NEW PERSONALIZED real estate coupon book. If the payment is being made by mail, simply tear out the coupon and enclose it with your check to the Mortgage Loan Dept.

If you are also a checking account customer of ours receiving a monthly statement, your real estate payment will appear on your NEW combined statement; showing the distribution of the payment. At the end of the year you will receive a statement showing all payments as received. This statement will also reflect the disbursements made for taxes and insurance.

If you have any questions concerning this new benefit, please contact the Mortgage Loan Department. We appreciate your continued patronage.

Sincerely yours,

Real Estate Department

LETTER TO REAL ESTATE BROKERS

LETTER A-35

Build goodwill that wins new customers from a special group of clients. A year-end customer relations letter.

Dear Real Estate Broker:

Trust is one of the acknowledged foundations of business. At ABC Bank, we believe friendship should be another. We are especially reminded of this as we reflect on the year just ended.

The friendship you have shown us throughout the year, and the trust you have placed in ABC Bank by recommending our association to your real estate buyers is sincerely appreciated. You have helped make this year an impressive growth for us and we are truly grateful for the part you played.

Your friends at ABC Bank join me in extending best wishes to you for a happy and bountiful 19____.

Sincerely,

ENJOY YOUR BANK FINANCED HOME LETTER

LETTER A-36

After the closing, build prompt payment and good will with a follow-up letter.

Dear _____:

Enjoy your home!

Now that you have moved into your ABC Bank financed home, enjoy the pleasure and security of home ownership by:

- Having mortgage life insurance and disability insurance protection to cover your home loan in case the breadwinner should become disabled or deceased.
- Being prompt in payment of real estate taxes and property insurance premiums.
- Keeping your home in good repair. Your home is then worth more to you and to future buyers when you desire to sell.
- Contacting us if unexpected illnesses or other problems arise so we can be of assistance.

Above all, you and your family will want to join with thousands of others in the pride of ownership of your own home.

Cordially,

ABC Bank

EXPLAINING THE REAL ESTATE ESCROW ACCOUNT LETTER

LETTER A-37

Better customer relations is established with an explanation of the annual escrow account adjustment.

Dear Real Estate Mortgage Customer:

The terms of your FHA or VA mortgage require that the bank collect in advance of the due date, sufficient funds to pay the hazard insurance and property tax on your real estate. For your convenience, the amount required is included in your monthly payment and held by us in a non-interest bearing escrow account.

Each year, your escrow account is reviewed for any necessary changes. Enclosed is a copy of the review which may require a change in the amount required to pay insurance premiums, taxes and assessments on your real estate.

The amount of the escrow account shortage, if any, may be paid in a lump sum if you wish. We will then notify you of your new lower payment amount upon receipt of the shortage sum.

It is our pleasure to be of assistance to you with any of our banking services.

Cordially,

BANK INTRODUCES A NEW FAMILY
TO THE NEIGHBORS LETTER

LETTER A-38

In small towns, banking can be very personal. This gives the small town bank a competitive edge over larger, less personal institutions operating from the more distant city.

Dear Neighbor:

We are delighted . . . to have been of service in our Real Estate and Executive Transfer Department to . . .

Mr. and Mrs. John Doe and family. Formerly of Anytown, New York, the Doe's have just moved into the house at 1111 Any Street. We know you'll want to meet them and they'll want to meet you, too. All of us at the ABC Bank would appreciate your making them feel welcome to our town.

Our Real Estate Department is ready to be of service to you, also, if the opportunity arises.

Cordially,

APOLOGY FOR A TAX ERROR BILLING
REAL ESTATE MORTGAGE LETTER

LETTER A-39

The bank sent the tax billing duplicate to the real estate owner requesting the tax to be paid directly, when it was supposed to be paid from the escrow account set up for that purpose.

Dear _____:

Thank you for calling about the tax billing instruction we sent.

We cannot understand why the ABC real estate billing clerk sent the tax duplicate bill to you in the first place. Please accept our apology for the error.

It certainly is a confusing error for us to make—especially since the taxes were paid by us directly to the County Treasurer on your behalf; the day BEFORE sending you the notice. Rest assured that the taxes on your property are paid and that your escrow account properly reflects this transaction.

Again, thank you for calling the error to our attention.

Very truly yours,

THANK YOU FOR YOUR REAL ESTATE MORTGAGE LETTER

LETTER A-40

A letter sent by a bank prior to closing that generates smooth closings and builds customer loyalty.

Dear New Homeowner:

We are pleased to inform you that your loan was approved for your real estate transaction.

All preprocessing has been completed and a closing date is scheduled for _____ at _____ A.M./P.M.

The remaining downpayment and closing costs needed to be paid by you at the closing is $_____.

The ABC Bank is pleased to be of service to you in real estate financing. An additional temporary loan fund has been approved for your use in the amount of $1,000.

Since many families want to add improvements or modernize the property shortly after moving in, this loan fund is available for 90 days after the closing date. It is available without further red-tape, as an installment loan, should you have need for it. This is ABC Bank's way of doing more for you as your bank.

We look forward to seeing you at the closing.

Sincerely,

THE FINAL REAL ESTATE PAYMENT LETTER

LETTER A-41

Build better banking relations by thanking the customer when the final payment is made.

Dear _____:

This is certainly a special occasion for you!

Your final real estate payment has been processed by ABC Bank, and enclosed are the cancelled mortgage papers.

After all the years in working toward liquidating your mortgage, we want to take this moment to express our appreciation for your prompt payment record. We are always delighted when we can aid our customers to eventually own their own home— FREE AND CLEAR.

Should you desire a new real estate financing plan for any reason—a vacation home or investment property—please contact us. We will provide you with an excellent mortgage service.

Best wishes.

ABC BANK

SELLER OF BANK MORTGAGE REAL ESTATE LETTER

LETTER A-42

The real estate mortgage is cancelled by sale of property cross-selling, and customer relations benefits are stressed in this goodwill letter.

Dear _____:

Your real estate agent has informed us that your property has been sold. The ABC Bank real estate mortgage payoff balance will be computed and given to the title company handling the final closing.

We want to express our thanks for the fine manner in which you have maintained the excellent payment schedule for your property.

If the ABC Bank can be of service in any banking need, you may be sure that we are willing to assist. Should you decide on a new property purchase, please remember that we want to be of service in any necessary real estate financing. You are a preferred customer.

Perhaps many of our other services can be useful to you at this time; such as notary service, trust department service, or even investment management. If we can offer any assistance, please call upon us.

Cordially,

STREAMLINED REAL ESTATE MORTGAGES LETTER

LETTER A-43

Tie-in a "Thank you" with benefit services to retain old customers and win new ones.

Dear Real Estate Broker:

We have streamlined our whole procedure of handling home loans. It is now designed to help your customers get into that dream home with less red tape and SOONER than before.

Our streamlined service means faster closings and shorter processing time from application date to closing date. It is our way of saying "Thank you" for your past patronage.

Your customers will receive competitive annual percentage rates. Our automatic payment plan from their checking account to the real estate loan account makes payments simple at ABC Bank.

Any ABC Bank branch can now process real estate applications in the evenings until 7 P.M. for your customer's convenience. Call us for the fastest conventional loan processing service in town.

You will be pleased with our streamlined real estate mortgages.

Cordially,

"CONSULT WITH US" TRUST LETTER

LETTER A-44

Build strong customer relations by informing the customer of the useful benefits of banking.

Dear _____:

As a friend and customer of the ABC Bank, you are entitled to consult with our Trust Department on important issues concerning your future. If you have not looked into this service, we invite you to take advantage of the information which has been provided for your benefit.

No one person at the ABC Bank handles all aspects of banking and finance. That is why we provide a Trust Department, with specialists who are qualified by experience and training to handle estates, wills and any of your trust requirements.

Enclosed is a brief folder that explains the special nature of our Trust Department and how you may benefit from Trust services. Your bank has an interest in your progress and stands ready to assist in your banking and trust requirements.

Cordially,

TRUST DEPARTMENT ANNUAL REVIEW LETTER

LETTER A-45

A good customer relations letter to accompany the statistical data from the Trust Department.

Dear _____:

At this time of the year, the ABC Bank Trust Department likes to pause and reflect on progress of the trust agreement during the past year. Your trust account analysis is enclosed for your review, along with the pertinent highlights that are significant for future performance.

We are pleased to inform you that the trust account has shown favorable growth in strict accord with your instructions. The coming year is expected to be one of stable growth in the economy, and your portfolio mix presently reflects this philosophy.

The ABC Bank Trust Department wishes you a safe and happy New Year.

Cordially,

INVESTMENT BANKING REVIEW LETTER

LETTER A-46

A customer relations letter that personalizes the investment banking relationship with a view towards solidifying a long-term association.

Dear _____:

It was just four years ago that you consulted with the ABC Bank Trust Department concerning your investment portfolio. I recall how worried and concerned you were about handling the diverse real estate and stock investments left to your management in your husband's will.

I still recall your comment after returning from the "get away from it" Hawaiian Cruise. When we chatted last week, you seemed much more at ease about the trust portfolio than you were at that difficult meeting four years ago when we first reviewed the lifetime trust. You touched on that point in our conversation last week. I am so happy that our Trust Department has been able to provide you with the lost investment expertise that was unique to your late husband; especially now that you feel secure in our handling of your trust portfolio.

I have enclosed the information on the adjustment in the portfolio mix as we discussed, and will be pleased to provide any further information you desire. Have a pleasant trip on your return to the Hawaiian Cruise next month.

Cordially,

Trust Department

A TRUST "THANK YOU FOR BANKING" GIFT LETTER

LETTER A-47

Build your customer relations by offering inexpensive free gifts to established Trust Department customers.

Dear _____:

It is yours free . . . from the ABC Trust Department. When we saw the enclosed snap-apart Key Holder, the Trust Department felt you would enjoy receiving a useful gift.

The Key Holder can protect your property. Whenever you are required to leave the automobile ignition key, you will be able to easily unsnap the Key Holder, permitting you to take your other valuable keys with you.

Just another way the ABC Bank can say, "Thank you for banking with us."

Cordially,

Trust Department

NEW AUTOMATED TRUST OPERATIONS LETTER

LETTER A-48

With new technology and data systems, the bank has an excellent opportunity to improve the customer relations' benefits.

Dear Customer:

The ABC Bank has completed a major improvement in trust operations. Now, the information available to Trust Department customers has been expanded to provide more timely and varied reporting as a result of the conversion to a fully automated system.

For the first time, the Trust Department can capture and retain unique and diverse investment facts that can place your trust manager in a more advantageous decision-making position.

The best opportunities for the future growth of trust funds lie in ABC's ability to expand its information reporting capacity. We feel you will appreciate the benefits of the new system.

Cordially,

CONGRATULATIONS TO A TRUST CUSTOMER LETTER

LETTER A-49

Customers of trust departments occasionally get in the news. A letter of congratulations enhances the customer relations aspect of banking.

Dear _____ :

We just read the newspaper report about the wonderful honor that has been bestowed upon you by the University. Certainly, an honorary Doctor's Degree is a unique and special recognition for your contribution to the business community.

We at the ABC Bank are especially proud to know you and count you as a customer of the bank and the Trust Department. When we review your trust portfolio in several months, we hope you can tell us more about your inventive contribution.

You have our best wishes for success and happiness.

Cordially,

GROUP *B* LETTERS

Sixty-Five Bank Marketing Letters That Increase Profit and Volume

- 11 Profit-oriented Commercial Banking Letters
- 10 Volume Producing Institutional Banking Letters
- 22 Innovative Retail Banking Letters
- 8 Real Estate Service Marketing Letters
- 14 Trust and Investment Marketing Incentive Letters

As customer relations is the heart of banking, the marketing of banking services in a competitive society is the lifeblood of the bank. In our evolving paperless bank transaction systems, banks are relying heavily on written communication to maintain or improve the share of the market presently enjoyed. The B Group of letters are selected for that powerful mission of garnering increased profits and volume for the bank.

Marketing letters are so important to a bank that they can result in producing thousands or even millions of dollars of added and new business. The opportunities to market banking services are endless. Some banks contacted present customers with statement stuffers; some blanketed selected neighborhoods; some contacted newcomers to the area; some wrote to potential newcomers; and some creatively "dreamed up" outstanding marketing programs that gave the bank an edge on offering new services—such as, direct deposit of security checks. Competing for the consumer market in retail banking opened new adventures for banks with loans, bank credit cards and innovative trust services.

The 65 Group B marketing letters provide built-in programs that can capture new business for the bank. The planning of each letter offers some of the best in marketing bank services.

"THERE'S A NEW INDUSTRY MOVING TO TOWN" LETTER

LETTER B-1

A profit-oriented commercial banking letter that garnered a new major business account for the bank.

> Dear _____:
>
> At the Chamber of Commerce it was said, "There's a new industry moving to town!" The ABC Bank is delighted it is you.
>
> There are many facts that support your decision. Our central market location, our skilled work force, our unmatched transportation system and our healthy attitude toward your type of business.
>
> The ABC Bank has available at your disposal many fine banking services: low-cost payroll processing, expert tax and financial advisors, unique business line-of-credit loans and special marketing services for business that can mean extra profits for you.
>
> We hope we can be of service—even before you become fully operational in your area. I have asked our Mr. _____ to give you a call of welcome and provide any assistance you may need.
>
> Sincerely,
>
> President
> ABC Bank

"WELCOME TO THE CORPORATE CLUB" MARKETING LETTER

LETTER B-2

An innovative marketing letter that is effective in cross-selling additional commercial banking services.

Dear Business Customer:

WELCOME TO THE CLUB . . .

It's always nice to send a friendly "hello" to the executive responsible for opening new corporate checking accounts with ABC Bank. Perhaps this is just one of many corporate accounts you have opened with us, but if it is your first account, we want to welcome you to the many banking services available at ABC Bank.

Our older corporate customers have found many advantages in our liberal consideration of business loans, leasehold improvement loans and even our unique equipment leasing program.

Now that you are a member of the ABC "Club" you are entitled to free notary service at any branch, use of our private conference rooms for special meetings (by appointment), and the counsel of all our bank officers in solving your banking and financial needs.

Wishing you good fortune in all your business plans.

Sincerely,

President
ABC Bank

GETTING A SHARE OF THE MARKET MERCHANT LETTER

LETTER B-3

This letter, combined with a follow-up letter, resulted in one bank's gaining more than 50 percent of the bank credit card merchant business. The balance of the market was divided among three competing banks.

Dear Merchant:

The ABC Bank is now offering the _____ bank credit card plan. We would like to share this business service with you.

Our plans include sending a mailer to our banking friends and customers in order to invite them to use our bank credit card plan. As you know, this card is valuable from coast-to-coast with an interchange between most of the key banks in the country.

Surveys have convinced us that credit customers buy four times as much from merchants offering this credit plan, as compared to cash customers. We think that the ABC Bank should promote this excellent benefit on your behalf.

The use of a bank credit card is profitable to the merchants that have used bank cards. Please complete the enclosed card, and we will send you the details about making easier and more sales for your business.

Cordially,

GETTING A SHARE OF THE MARKET FOLLOW-UP LETTER

LETTER B-4

This follow-up letter clinched the wavering merchants in the marketing plan.

Dear Merchant:

Frankly we're disappointed that you did not respond to the ABC Bank Credit Card Marketing Program initiated with our earlier announcement.

At this time, over 1,000 area merchants have now signed with us to offer the bank credit card. However, without your prestigious name on the list of merchants offering the ABC plan, the consumer may be disappointed. Our multimedia promotion plans call for a complete list of merchants accepting our card to be mailed to area residents. Surely you'll want your retail business included in this group.

Also, our representative will offer suggestions for your promotional tie-in that will garner added business for you. Sign the enclosed card and mail it today. Our representative wants to go to work on your marketing plan immediately.

Sincerely,

President
ABC Bank

OFFERING INTERNATIONAL BANKING SERVICES LETTER

LETTER B-5

Citing the essential benefits of the international banking service brought several profitable commercial accounts to a bank of moderate size.

Dear Mr. _____:

Your comments yesterday about international banking certainly express the current consensus on the complex economic conditions around the globe.

The International Banking Division of the ABC Bank offers a highly skilled banking service to businesses. We recognize the growing importance of foreign trade to our community. For example, our area ranks among the top 30 exporting centers in the United States. This means that one out of every 18 job-holding residents is involved with export-related activity (according to the Chamber of Commerce report).

The ABC Bank, with a staff of specialists, is in a position to handle your international banking functions. If you like, I will introduce you to Mr. _____, Executive Vice-President of our International Department. Stop by the bank tomorrow, and you can have an opportunity to pick the brains of the best international banker in town.

Sincerely,

COMMERCIAL ENERGY CRISIS LOANS

LETTER B-6

Existing commercial checking account customers receiving this letter responded with eight million dollars in loan requests.

Dear _____:

As a valued customer of ABC Bank, we want to offer a unique service for your business which will ease the worry of future energy crisis shutdowns.

We have developed a Special Energy Crisis Loan just for commercial customers. We will work with your contractor to determine energy saving improvements in your business. Once you and the contractor agree upon a program, we will offer a lower interest loan over an extended time period, customized to your particular needs and requirements.

Contact our special Energy Crisis Loan Officer at ABC Bank for further information and application. You will be glad you did.

Sincerely,

NEW MERCHANT BANK CARD LETTER

LETTER B-7

A commercial banking marketing letter for the bank card business.

Gentlemen:

Thank you for becoming an important part of ABC Bank's family of credit card businesses. Your charge card needs and those of your customers are answered by this one convenient and re-spected card service.

Now that you have signed on with ABC Bank we look forward to serving you in many ways. You will find us responsive to all your credit card and commercial needs—from loans to payroll checking.

We appreciate your business and look forward to a long-term relationship.

If you have any questions about _____ Credit Card, or any of our many banking services, please call me, anytime.

Sincerely,

President

LEASING CAPITAL EQUIPMENT MARKET LETTER

LETTER B-8

This letter generated over two million dollars in new leasing contracts for the bank.

Dear Customer:

Now, for the first time in Middle America you can lease capital equipment directly from your bank. Machine tools, forklifts, executive aircraft, hospital equipment, materials handling equipment . . . whatever you need in the way of capital equip-ment, we are ready to lease it to you.

ADVANTAGES OF DIRECT LEASING:

- Improve your cash flow
- Conserve your cash and working capital
- Acquire needed equipment immediately

WHY YOU SHOULD LEASE FROM ABC BANK:

When you lease through ABC Bank, we handle all the financial details. You do not have to spend valuable time arranging for credit. In addition, you deal with skilled lease experts, who have at their fingertips all the financial experience of more than 100 years of banking.

HERE'S HOW IT WORKS:

First you decide on the type of equipment you need; then establish specifications and costs. In other words, you do your own shopping. You tell us exactly what equipment you need, who you want to buy it from and how much it costs. Then, ABC Bank buys the equipment and leases it to you. You have complete use of it; just as if you were the owner.

You can lease just about any kind of capital equipment from ABC Bank. You name it—any kind of *production* or *processing* equipment, from one item to a plant-full. The only exceptions are real property and transportation equipment for personal use.

TERMS AND CONDITIONS:

ABC Bank, as owner and Lessor, enters into a written lease agreement with you as the Lessee; under which you agree to make periodic rental payments to ABC Bank over the period of the lease. Generally, the lease period equals the approximate useful life of the equipment. At the end of the lease period, you may continue to rent the equipment for greatly reduced rentals; or the Bank will trade in the equipment and replace it with new equipment according to your specifications.

Your first step should be to consult with your legal, tax and accounting advisors to determine the benefits of leasing. Then contact the Manager of the Leasing Section at ABC Bank, or call your Commercial Loan Officer.

Yours very truly,

Equipment Leasing Dept.

UNDERSTANDING THE BUSINESS FINANCIAL SITUATION LETTER

LETTER B-9

An innovative marketing letter that emphasizes a team of commercial specialists who serve the banking needs of corporate clients.

Dear Mr. Business President:

We make it our business to develop an understanding of corporate customer banking needs. Our bank officers are able to develop plans that organize the banking resources for your maximum use.

Beginning with simple credit accommodations, we are able to develop a wide range of banking services that help you succeed. The ABC Bank staff can provide commercial lending, construction lending, equipment leasing, corporate trust services, cash management and short-term investment of excess cash.

Whatever your financial concern today, share it with one of our bank officers who can offer over 100 bank services tailored for your business. Call us today and we'll go to work for you.

Cordially,

COMMERCIAL BANK FINANCING PRIOR TO GOVERNMENT APPROVAL LETTER

LETTER B-10

Dear _____:

Your report and analysis of the manufacturing of gas turbines as part of a contract with the Navy has been carefully reviewed by our executive board. We appreciate the extensive summary of your short-term financial needs while the Navy evaluates your report and proposal.

Since you are a long-time customer with an admirable financial record, the executive committee has agreed to underwrite the short-term financing required by you. Certainly, the 3,700 employees of your firm have an immense stake in the success of your proposal, as does the entire community.

Please stop by my office at your earliest convenience so the proper documents can be completed for the financial accommodation.

Sincerely,

Executive Vice-President

JOINT VENTURE INVESTMENT LETTER

LETTER B-11

A profit-oriented marketing concept that proposes a joint venture rather than the traditional wholly-owned manufacturing facilities.

Dear _____:

Now that you have made the decision to invest in the manufacturing facilities as proposed, you need to consider whether or not the wholly-owned independent subsidiary is the best form of financial stability.

It is the opinion of some of us around the bank, that your new venture be undertaken in partnership with another company. Before making your final decision, consider several important factors that might outweigh the possible disadvantages of a joint venture.

A joint venture could provide valuable knowledge of highly competitive marketing. Teaming with a company that has dynamic management in the special marketing area of new manufacturing facilities will provide a solid entrance into instant sales. Your operations could be profitable in a shorter time frame, than if you had started totally new ones.

Under the joint venture concept, we are in a stronger position to invest in your securities and to grant substantial financial accommodations to the new subsidiary. If you would like to review several alternatives using us as a "sounding board" for the new facilities, please give me a call. Best wishes for a successful marketing program.

Cordially,

HOW TO BECOME A MILLIONAIRE MARKETING LETTER

LETTER B-12

This letter has sparked the growth of one bank from 10.1 million dollars to 14.9 million in assets in less than two years.

Dear Resident:

We're changing our image! Won't you join us and be a mini-millionaire, too? Yes . . . we're just a small bank that wants success and growth. We know we will need partners who also have dreams of fame and fortune, and want you as our partner!

The ABC Bank has a Millionaire's Starter Kit available for you. Simply open a savings account with as little as one dollar and the Millionaire's Starter Kit is yours, free.

Follow the Millionaire's Savings Plan by filling the dime saver, and in just a few short weeks you will have saved $100—all from your loose dimes. Bring your Millionaire's Starter Kit filled with dimes, to the bank and deposit them in a savings account. Then . . . watch it grow . . . as you fill more Millionaire's Starter Kits. With each completed kit deposited in your savings account—either a new or existing one—you are eligible for one chance for the drawing. A $250 addition to your Millionaire Savings Account from your partner—ABC Bank.

So hurry on down to see us and pick up your Millionaire's Starter Kit, partner.

Cordially,

ABC Bank

P.S. Don't spend any dimes for a while.

JUST ANOTHER "KID" ON THE BLOCK LETTER

LETTER B-13

An unusual institutional letter that resulted in new banking business.

Dear Customer:

We are just another "kid" on the block!

It has been six years since we opened our branch at _____ Street, and we are still kids. We hope you are pleased with our young banking services.

If you have not considered our business loans, as the need arises don't hesitate to talk to one of our branch officers. Even though we have been on the block only six years, we can call on big brother downtown for the heavy funds needed for business.

The ABC Bank is pleased to be of service to you at any time.

Cordially,

Branch Manager

CONVENIENCE IN BANKING LETTER

LETTER B-14

An institutional letter that improves the marketing of total bank services.

Dear _____:

At ABC Bank, we have long known that the key factor in attracting new customers is banking convenience.

As we open our seventh branch office, ABC Bank is closer to more homes than ever before. Most potential bank customers believe, according to a survey, that "near home" is the best definition of convenience. Added branch offices permit ABC's banking staff to be more closely identified with the neighborhood we serve.

You will frequently find our branch managers outside the branch office, working closely with neighborhood customers to provide banking services.

We hope you are pleased with the added convenience in banking provided at ABC Bank. Your requests for banking services make it our desire to provide more convenience.

Cordially,

INSTITUTIONAL SELLING OF FULL BANKING SERVICES LETTER

LETTER B-15

Stress the strength of the bank as an institution and watch the customers' confidence result in increased banking volume.

Dear _____:

You opened a checking and savings account with us two months ago. We hope our staff has acquainted you with the many services provided for customers.

This has been an extraordinary year for banking. Because of the five city leaders who organized the ABC Bank in 1890 with solid financial planning, we are today blessed with strong and healthy growth based on conservative, profitable loan policies. The ninety-five men and women now employed take pride in their performance and in the satisfaction of doing a good job.

The ABC Bank is at your service day and night. Should you wish to discuss a business or financial problem, opportunity to purchase real estate, need for a new automobile or a personal loan, please feel free to talk to any of your banking friends at the ABC Bank. We are here for the purpose of working with you.

With full use of your banking services, you can make it possible to enjoy the better things in life. We want to see you in the bank, regularly.

Cordially,

President

CONTEST TO ANNOUNCE NEW BRANCH OFFICE LETTER

LETTER B-16

This resident mailer generated 942 new savings accounts, 2,417 new checking accounts and 112 new loan applications.

Dear Resident:

Now there's an ABC Bank branch office near you—at _____ Street. It's a small, friendly office equipped to handle all your banking needs.

To celebrate our opening, each day during opening week our guests will receive souvenir pens. In addition, you may register for one of the three weekend vacations to be awarded on May 10. Yes, *three* lucky winners will receive one of the following dream weekends as the guest of ABC Bank:

- New York's famous spots . . . a great weekend for two with round trip air fare, two nights at a top hotel and your choice of shows and dinners at famous New York night spots.
- The Washington D.C. Capitol thrill . . . a stimulating weekend for two with round trip air fare, two nights at a Hilton Hotel and a choice of special tours.
- The Family Relaxer . . . a real vacation for the entire family at the renown Country Club. Enjoy three days and two nights at this scenic retreat featuring family entertainment—swimming, golf, tennis, bowling or horseback riding.

All arrangements for prize weekends will be made by a travel agency. Winners may select any weekend between now and December 31.

YOU NEED NOT BE PRESENT TO WIN!

STEAK SWEEPSTAKES CONTEST LETTER

LETTER B-17

An introduction to a bank branch in a supermarket, with a get-acquainted contest that garnered 480 new bank customers.

Dear Neighbor:

Now you can bank while you shop for dinner!

We want to introduce you to the newest ABC Bank Branch at the _____ Supermarket.

Our "Steak Sweepstakes" offers you a chance to win valuable gift certificates worth from $10 to $100 in groceries at the Supermarket. There's nothing to buy to enter. Simply fill out the entry blank and drop it in the box at our new office in the Supermarket.

Twenty-seven lucky people will be winners and one might be you. Hurry and enter today!

The "Steak Sweepstakes" is our way of introducing you to the little bank in the grocery. We are trying to make banking more convenient for you.

Cordially,

ANNOUNCING A SECRET KEY TO BANKING SERVICE LETTER

LETTER B-18

A general announcement that brought in 327 loan applications for a moderate-sized bank.

Dear Customer:

With the advent of the newest, most modern service in the banking industry, we are providing an additional service.

The ABC Bank proudly announces _____ Bank Credit Card with a Mag Stripe, the secret key to better banking for you. In the event you have not already received your _____ Card, please complete the questionnaire on the enclosed brochure, drop it in the mail, and you will soon be carrying with you the handiest and newest banking card.

Very truly yours,

ABC Bank

"BUSINESS IS LOOKING UP" LETTER

LETTER B-19

An optimistic letter from a small bank that generated personal enthusiasm and $142,000 in new loan volume in four months.

Dear Resident:

The economic news is beginning to take on a brighter future as economists return to talk of sustainable growth. There is definitely a feeling that business is looking up.

Major research firms indicate that a larger percentage of businesses have definite plans to expand their operations. Our own area research indicates that the consumer assisted in the recovery, and will continue to buy as a result of higher incomes and continuing affluence.

Perhaps you plan to take advantage of the spring weather, by helping business perk up with a modernization purchase, new automobile or household purchase. Remember, the ABC Bank wants to help you if a loan is needed. Stop at our office when you are downtown and review our many ways to assist with spring purchases.

Sincerely,

OUR BANKING SPANS THE WORLD LETTER

LETTER B-20

An institutional banking letter that emphasizes the world-wide solidarity of banking relationships.

Dear Mr. Businessman:

Outside the major money centers, there is a growing demand for international banking services. The multi-national corporation finds international services a must, as do smaller firms dealing with the multi-national or supplying sophisticated manufactured subcomponents.

The activities of ABC Bank's International Division currently span the world; with a network of over 200 correspondent banks in foreign countries and deposit relationships with banks in over 15 major countries.

When your financial banking needs require international handling, call us in. We can be very helpful.

Cordially,

CREATIVE BANKING SERVICES GARNER NEW BUSINESS LETTER

LETTER B-21

Generate new business with the consultant's viewpoint of banking service. One bank brought in a $110,000 new deposit with this letter.

Dear Customer:

The success of any bank depends primarily on the sustained growth of the customers being served. To ensure customer growth, ABC Bank officers work closely with businesses as consultants and creative solvers of financial money needs.

If you are not taking advantage of all our many banking services, we invite you to talk with a bank officer about the innovative ways in which we can create financial solutions to old business problems. Perhaps our International Department can assist in a difficult foreign bid situation or our Real Estate Department can solve a construction financing problem. Also, we can provide a variety of automated services—from funds transfer to complete payroll accounting—tailored specifically for your business.

Whatever your current needs, call us at ABC Bank. We may have just solved the same problem for another businessman.

Cordially,

"WHY CAN'T I SAVE LIKE . . . " LETTER

LETTER B-22

A unique letter that encourages new savings accounts from your checking account customers. One bank received a 14 percent response for new savers activation from existing checking account customers.

Dear Customer:

Have you ever asked, "Why can't I save like . . . everyone else?" When we were asked this question at ABC Bank, we found a solution. A simple, sensible way to save that's entirely free.

Just tell us how much you want to save each month, and that amount will be automatically transferred from your ABC Bank checking account into your ABC Savings Program. We make immediate deposits. You never have a moment's delay in receiving interest, and your account grows and earns interest from day of deposit to day of withdrawal; credited quarterly.

At ABC Bank we'll look after your savings program for you. Even if you're out of town or on vacation. We'll help you save regularly, which gives you savings success power.

Simply complete the enclosed savings coupon and we will help you to become richer and save like . . . everyone else.

ABC Bank

NEST EGG SAVINGS LETTER

LETTER B-23

A unique letter that encouraged additional time deposit savings accounts. This letter was used as a checking account statement mail stuffer. The response was 12 percent of the mailing.

ABC Bank introduces its extra large time deposit savings account!

NOW—Gather your Extra Large Nest Egg.

We guarantee you will receive this interest: 7.90% effective yield on 7.50% for the time agreed upon. Your minimum deposit of $1,000 for maturity dates of six years to ten years.

WHY IS THIS SO GREAT?

When you open this NEST EGG, you will receive the newest, highest legal rate now allowed us by Federal Regulations. In today's fluctuating world of money rates, this is one of the more secure investments for you.

Be a wise owl and pick the extra large NEST EGGS, the best in town.

(Federal laws and regulations prohibit the payment of a time deposit, prior to maturity or stated withdrawal periods, without substantial loss of interest. Interest on the amount withdrawn is reduced to the passbook rate.)

ABC Bank

NEWCOMER PROMOTION LETTER

LETTER B-24

A helping hand plus a trying situation equals more bank customers.

Dear _____:

Deciding to move is hard enough, not to mention all the details involved in relocating. Why not let ABC Bank share some of the load?

Upon your arrival, we can have your free checking account and daily interest savings account opened and ready for use, at our branch located conveniently close to your new home. Just complete the enclosed signature cards, return them to us and we'll take it from there. It's one less thing for you to worry about and one more thing we can do for you!

Our Branch Officer, _____, is eager to meet you, so stop by and introduce yourself when you're settled or call him at (000) 123-4567. He can explain all the other banking services we provide, including: free checking, 5% savings compounded daily, American Express Gold Card, Bank Credit Card, Cash Reserve (overdraft protection), and a wide range of personal loans tailored to fit your budget and your relocation needs.

Let us be your guide to good fortune in the metropolitan area.

Sincerely yours,

Senior Vice-President

BANK TRANSFER SERVICES LETTER

LETTER B-25

A unique letter sent after initial inquiry by a customer planning to move to your community from another area.

Dear New Neighbor:

Thank you for your interest in ABC Bank. We'll be happy to be your bank in the _____ metropolitan area. We offer a wide variety of services—and more.

Simply complete the enclosed transfer information card and the signature cards. Use the pre-addressed, postage-paid envelope to speed the information to us for processing.

After you arrive in the city:

- Order permanent checks at the local branch or telephone us at _____.
- We will forward your Bank Credit Card to your new home.

- Your former Credit Card Relationship may be dissolved by cutting the old card in half, and mailing it to your former bank. If there is an outstanding balance, get a cash advance at any of the thirty-four branch offices for the outstanding amount. Send a check, your statement and the cut credit card to your old bank. Your former bank credit card account will be closed and the outstanding balance will be present on your ABC Bank Credit Card Statement.

- If you have any questions about your savings or checking account transfer procedure, please call us at _____. Yes, we welcome your collect call.

We want to make your move as pleasant as possible.

Cordially,

SOCIAL SECURITY DIRECT DEPOSIT LETTER

LETTER B-26

The marketing letter that spurs forward the EFTS concept and a new banking service.

Dear _____:

NOW . . . YOU CAN HAVE YOUR SOCIAL SECURITY CHECK MAILED DIRECTLY TO . . . your ABC Bank Checking Account—and we'll guarantee your deposit, even if the mail is late.

We deposit your funds in your account on the third of each month, even if ABC doesn't receive your check on time. The money is yours—*guaranteed*!

Thirty to 90 days may be required for the government to process your direct deposit. So your first check will be deposited to your ABC Bank Account the day we receive it. After that it's automatic—and *guaranteed*!

This service provides you with:

- *Safety*—no more chance of stolen or lost checks.
- *Convenience*—no trips to cash your check in bad weather.
- *No delays*—no missing or late checks, even if you change your address.
- *Money in the bank*—even when you're ill, on vacation or simply if you have better things to do than cash a check.

Stop in at any of our convenient locations. We'll help you fill out the U.S. Government form for direct deposit of your Social Security check.

ABC Bank

INNOVATIVE BANKING DIRECT DEPOSIT LETTER

LETTER B-27

This innovative Social Security Direct deposit bank service is presented with five customer benefits. This tested letter was found to be highly successful—780 new savings accounts and 1,846 checking deposits—for the bank sending this market promotion letter.

Dear _____ :

We are announcing a NEW service that the _____ Bank now offers.

Direct deposit in either a Savings Account or a Checking Account of your monthly Social Security check may now be made with your approval.

This new service will offer you many ADVANTAGES.

For example, by having your check deposited directly into a Savings Account, the deposit will begin earning interest IMMEDIATELY—without having to wait for you to make a special trip to the bank to cash your check and then make a deposit in person.

Our service will eliminate the problem for people who find it difficult to come to the bank to cash checks personally. By having the monthly Social Security check deposited directly into a _____ Bank Checking Account—you are able to pay a bill or get cash—simply by writing a check at any store or business.

The United States Government is adopting this nationwide Direct Deposit Program to Improve service to beneficiaries, to Reduce forgeries and thefts of checks, and to Lower government costs in the issuance of the monthly Social Security checks.

All you need to do to take advantage of this new bank service is to sign a simple application card. If you have further questions about our new service, any of the people in the bank will be happy to discuss the Social Security Direct Deposit.

Yours very truly,

Executive Vice-President

"IT'S FREE, NEIGHBOR"—TRY NEW SERVICES LETTER

LETTER B-28

An outstanding cross-selling banking letter that "flooded" the bank with new business.

Dear Neighbor:

At ABC, we are trying hard to be the friendliest bank in town. That's why we've added two new services: Free Checking and Daily Interest on savings.

Free Checking means you can write as many checks as you want, without being charged a cent for the service. This saves you money every month, and saves you time and confusion when it's time to balance your checkbook.

Compounded Daily Interest means you start to collect 5% earnings on your ABC Savings Account from the very first day, and you keep on earning interest every day. Since the interest is compounded, you earn interest today on the interest you earned yesterday. So your money builds on itself!

Stop by our ABC Bank Branch located at 1000 Town Road, or call me at 111-1000 and let me show you how our two new services can make banking better for you.

Sincerely,

Branch Officer

SELLING FINGERTIP BANKING SERVICES LETTER

LETTER B-29

Introduces the debit card with innovative fingertip banking services that customers need in the future EFTS banking system.

Dear Mr. _____:

Now, ABC's Fingertip Banking offers anytime-anyplace banking. With little or no assistance you can transact your personal banking business day or night, on weekends or holidays . . . easily, quickly and privately.

Our New Fingertip Banking offers fast, "fingertip" convenience three ways. With SHOP'N TELLER machines at courtesy counters in selected stores, ANYTIME TELLERS at ABC Bank locations, and the TELLER PHONE—your own telephone.

Your ABC Card is the key to these FINGERTIP BANKING Services:

- *Deposits to Checking*
- *Deposits to Savings*
- *Withdrawals from checking*
- *Withdrawals from savings*
- *Transfer of funds between checking and savings*

To take advantage of SHOP'N TELLER and ANYTIME TELLER services, all you need is an ABC Bank Checking or Savings Account, and an ABC Card with your secret identification number. (It's mailed to you after you receive your ABC Card.)

There's no better time to apply for your Fingertip Card than today. So just fill out the enclosed postage-paid return card and drop it in the mail. You'll be hearing from us soon.

Cordially,

FREE TRIAL OFFER TO SWITCH BANKS LETTER

LETTER B-30

An exciting retail bank marketing program that cut heavily into the share of market competition. Over 1,000 new checking account applications were made in two weeks.

Dear Customer:

You will discover twenty-six reasons to use ABC Banking . . . to prove it, we want you to enjoy a THREE MONTH FREE TRIAL OFFER* on our Alphabet Account—our most valuable checking account, with all these "super extras": unlimited checking, personalized checks, overdraft protection (if you qualify), 10% off installment loan costs, no fees on traveler's checks, cashier's checks or money orders, 24-hour banking, the first dollar in your savings account, and notary service. Plus eighteen additional services.

At ABC Bank, you are the one! And we'd like you to be the judge when it comes to the best checking account value in town . . . the Alphabet Account.

In fact, we're so convinced that you'll be entirely pleased with all the services of the Alphabet Account, that we'll give you an account for three months at absolutely no cost to you.

At the end of three months, if you wish to continue the account, it will cost you only $2.89 a month for all the services listed above. Compare that with your present checking account and we think you'll be the one to switch to an Alphabet Account.

Trial offer for opening a new Alphabet Account ends September 10.

Cordially,

*This means you will not be charged the $2.89 monthly service fee on your first three monthly statements.

BANKING WITH AUTOMATED TELLER MACHINES LETTER

LETTER B-31

An innovative retail marketing letter that generated a 38 percent response for additional services from existing customers.

Dear Customer:

Did you know that when you have a checking or savings account with ABC Bank, you can transact business at any ABC Bank office or remote teller?

Any one of our Personal Bankers or Automated Teller Machines can provide you service near your home, work, or place of shopping. In fact, our newest "Banker" is our Automated Teller, now being installed at each branch as well as in many supermarkets and retail stores in the area. Our reason is simple—we want to make banking services more convenient for you.

Now, late at night or early in the morning, you can make deposits, withdrawals in cash, pay utilities, pay loans and add to your savings. No more rush hours, deadlines, and waiting in long lines for you. Our new "Banker" will keep your transactions confidential—and *even* give you a receipt!

If you're not using all our services—you should allow us to formally introduce you to our newest "Banker." Stop in at any branch, so you can receive your personal "introduction card" to our Automated Banker.

Cordially,

SELLING THE DEBIT CARD PACKAGE LETTER

LETTER B-32

Introducing combined retail banking services is consumer-oriented and attracts customers as well as more volume.

Dear Customer:

The newly introduced SUPER Account provides all the personal banking services you're likely to need, in one complete package for just $3 a month and *No Minimum Balance*.

Your ABC Bank SUPER Account is a whole new approach to banking. It's designed to make your personal banking even easier at ABC. We think it's the best banking bargain you'll find anywhere in the state. Now you can get eight basic personal banking services plus your own SUPER ID card, all for the single monthly fee of $3; and with no minimum balance requirement.

Look at all you get for just $3:

1. Free checking
2. Free checks: Pre-numbered and personalized with your name and address. A *super* idea.
3. Reduced Loan Rates
4. No-fee Traveler's Checks
5. Free Safe Deposit Box
6. Bank Credit Card
7. Combined Statement
8. Sure-Growth Savings (Automatic transfer every month from your checking account.)
9. SUPER Account Debit Card

   The SUPER Account card identifies you as a customer, entitled to many privileges and special savings.

For easy banking at ABC Bank get your SUPER Account today. Come see us, or call us at _____. Better yet, complete and mail the application form.

Sincerely,

MEET YOUR NEW BANK CREDIT CARD LETTER

LETTER B-33

This letter, mailed to *homeowners* in the market area, brought in over 15,000 new applications.

Dear Neighbor:

Meet our new bank card!

It's the credit card that's as active as you are. Finally, a credit card that's big enough for YOUR way of life. Once you have a card, you won't need all those other credit cards that you had to carry around for years.

WELCOME everywhere; that's the new ABC BANK credit card!

_____ credit card is the biggest and best shopping and travel card, honored by over four million merchants. You can even get a cash advance at over 5,000 bank offices across the country. Better than money, our card is the one you'll want to carry everywhere.

APPLY NOW FOR YOUR ABC BANK CREDIT CARD. Enclosed is a brief application to complete and sign. Fold it over and seal. Just drop it in the mail and we pay postage. Then sit back and relax . . . shortly you'll be enjoying the newest credit card in town; once your application is approved.

ABC Bank

ADVANCE NOTICE OF NEW RETAIL BANKING SERVICE LETTER

LETTER B-34

This letter successfully opened over 2,000 new bank card accounts— each with a $1,000 credit line from a preselected customer file. The letter includes the customer name in the body of letter.

Dear _____:

Because you are a preferred customer of ABC Bank, we're giving you advance notice of a new ABC service—the ABC Account—and offering it to you without the need to fill out a credit application.

Even if you already have a Bank Card Account with another bank, you can now have an EXTRA CREDIT LINE of $1,000 just by accepting an ABC Bank Card. If you don't already have a _____ Credit Card, let me explain what it can mean to you.

It's a good feeling to have . . . . .Credit Card to count on in emergencies—for car repairs, medical and dental services, or unexpected travel. It's the most widely accepted card for dining, lodging, traveling and shopping around the world; as well as across town, at such respected stores as: _____, _____, _____. And . . . you can draw immediate cash advances from any ABC office, or any other _____ Credit Card bank in the world.

The billing method is simple and convenient. When your statement arrives, you'll find every transaction listed separately so that you can verify each item. You write only one check for payment—no matter how many purchases you've made. In addition, you won't find any annual dues or membership fees with _____ Bank Credit Card.

To receive your ABC CREDIT CARD, simply sign the enclosed Acceptance Certificate, drop it in the mail, and I'll see that the _____ family will be included as charter customers when we mail our first ABC Bank Credit Cards.

Welcome to ABC BANK CARD!

Sincerely,

ACCEPTANCE CERTIFICATE

LETTER B-34a

ABC BANK

An Invitation to Enjoy the Convenience of a Bank Credit Card

Customer name
Address

APPROVED FOR IMMEDIATE ISSUE

YES, I accept your invitation to become an ABC cardholder without the need to fill out a credit application.

Authorized Credit Line:$1,000

Please issue my card at once. *Signature* *Date*

Offer Expires: May 10, 19___

BANK CREDIT CARD—NEW MERCHANT PROMOTION LETTER

LETTER B-35

A unique credit card promotion letter that encouraged higher initial credit card activity and promoted awareness of a *new* major merchant, added to the expanding list of valuable merchants offered by a bank credit card. Results: in two months over $150,000 in new credit receivables from one new merchant.

Dear Cardholder:

We welcome the opportunity to serve you with an ABC Bank Credit Card.

You may conveniently charge future purchases at _____

store and other ABC Bank Credit Card merchants on your account.

Your bank credit card has no connection with any balance you may have on your department store account. Please make any payments due the store directly to your department store account, as you have done in the past.

This new service, the bank credit card, can now be used by you as an added shopping convenience at the department store. We hope you will enjoy the new service, and if you have any questions, please contact us at the bank.

Cordially,

Customer Services

FREE LICENSE PLATES PROMOTE AUTO LOANS LETTER

LETTER B-36

This loan promotion increased auto loan volume by 26 percent over the same period in the previous year.

Dear _____:

ABC Bank provides free license plates for your car.

We will pick up the tab for your 19____ plates or stickers if you buy a car before _____ and finance it through us. We'll even deliver your plates or stickers by mail! No lines—no hassle.

Our offer includes loans for new cars, used cars, trucks and boats. With a loan of $2,000 or more for a minimum of twelve months, the plates are on us.

Ask your dealer for details or stop by any of our fifteen offices. You can apply for a loan by telephone, too. Simply call our Loan Service at: (telephone number).

Yours for happy motoring,

TRADING OUR GIFT FOR YOUR AUTO LOAN
PROMOTION LETTER

LETTER B-37

Successful free gift promotion that increased seasonal auto loans by 19 percent.

Dear Customer:

At ABC Bank we do lots of things to help you through these days when every penny counts.

TAKE YOUR AUTO LOAN FOR INSTANCE.

We know you've really thought hard about the cost of buying a car. Come to ABC Bank during April, May or June because we are going to *give you a free gift* with a loan of $2,000 or more.

It's the Highway Emergency Kit. More than a superb $19.95 value! It is thoughtfully planned to help you through the many emergencies a motorist encounters. The kit contains items to solve problems on the spot, plus features that keep you safe during night driving breakdowns. Your kit is planned to save you, save money and save time. And then you're back on the road, driving!

The Highway Emergency Kit features:

- *Booster cables*
- *Tire inflator*
- *Emergency blinker*
- *Emergency first aid kit*
- *Aerosol-can fire extinguisher*

Simply fill out the enclosed application for your auto loan or bring it to your nearest bank branch.

Come to us for your auto loan—we want to help you on the road.

Sincerely,

AUTO LOAN CASH REBATE PROMOTION LETTER

LETTER B-38

An innovative marketing program that netted for one bank $17 million in loans in three months with 40 percent new customers.

Welcome to the ABC Bank!

During the next three months, you may be thinking about buying a new or used auto. We want to help you choose a new auto convenient for you and your family.

If you decide on a purchase of a *new* auto, any model or price, we want to offer you a cash rebate check of $50 if you finance your new auto with us.

Yes! A $50 cash rebate check is yours at the time the loan is delivered, if you let us be your car loan banker.

Simply fill out the auto loan application or visit one of our many branches. Once approved—tell us when you want to pick up your $50 check.

Sincerely,

FREE CHECKING ACCOUNT WITH AUTO LOAN PROMOTION LETTER

LETTER B-39

The bank branch that mailed this letter garnered a 50 percent increase in total loan volume!

Dear Neighbor:

Go ahead and get that new car this year! The friendliest bank in town now has the friendliest interest rates on new car loans. If you want to buy through our easy direct debit/bank plan, you qualify for our money-saving 9½% rate.

The best way for you to enjoy your low-rate auto loan, is to tie it in with a FREE ABC Bank Checking Account. You pick the car and make the deal; we provide you with the money. Your car payments are deducted from your account each month—no checks for you to write, no payment date to remember. What could be easier?

If you don't have FREE CHECKING at ABC Bank, stop by our Branch located at _____ Street, or call me at 111-1111 and let me show you what you're missing.

But remember, you are already qualified for our new low interest rate, whether you have an account with us or not. That's just our way of being friendly.

Sincerely,

Branch Manager

ENERGY CONSERVATION PROMOTION LETTER

LETTER B-40

This letter generated 800 new loan applications for energy conservation purposes.

Dear Friend:

Let us help you conserve energy!

At ABC Bank we are concerned about the energy shortage. We want to do our part to enable you to conserve energy and save money at the same time. During the next six months, we will reduce the cost of energy conservation loans for home and business by 1%.

Call us, or stop in for more details about extended payment plans for the lower cost energy conservation loans.

Very truly yours,

ENERGY CONSERVATION LETTER

LETTER B-41

Banking services that respond to a nation's energy crisis result in over 1,500 loan requests.

Dear Customer:

Now, at ABC Bank, you can save 2% of the interest rate on any energy conservation home improvement loan.

And—you can even wait 90 days after you receive the loan, before making the first loan payment.

You're probably faced with increased utility bills and some unforeseen expenses during the winter months. We want to help you keep your home warm and conserve energy at the same time. That's why we offer our lower terms on conservation home improvement loans.

ALL energy conservation loans qualify for our special 2% rate reduction and deferred payment. Consider those new storm windows, new insulation, roofing, siding, new water heater or an improved heating system.

Let us show you how to save money by making energy conservation improvements at your home or business.

Sincerely,

SELLING THE INSTALLMENT IMPROVEMENT LOAN LETTER

LETTER B-42

This letter increased new loan business 9 percent in 45 days.

Spring, 19____

SPRING AND THE ECONOMY ARE ON THE UPTURN.
A GOOD TIME TO IMPROVE YOUR PROPERTY.

These bright signs make it a little easier to decide which important repairs are best for your home. Or perhaps it's time to remodel the kitchen, add on a garage, or replace your worn-out stove or refrigerator.

These necessities don't go away—in good times or bad. Now with the future outlook a bit more cheerful, immediate home improvements make a lot of sense.

Remember, the longer you postpone repairs, remodelings, or purchases; the more expensive they will become. It's true. Rising costs make right now a more practical time to get started on home improvements. And, you'll get the satisfaction and conveniences you want and need, right away.

Check with an ABC Bank Loan Counselor who can help you get a head start on spring.

Very truly yours,

ENERGY REDUCING HOME IMPROVEMENT LOAN LETTER

LETTER B-43

Solving the weather crisis is innovative, no-nonsense banking service.

Dear Customer:

Who says we can't do anything about the weather?

At ABC Bank we want to help you keep your home warmer and conserve energy at the same time. Take advantage of the special Energy Reducing Home Improvement Loan. It's 2% lower in interest rate than our regular home improvement loans AND the first payment can be deferred for a full 90 days after the loan is made.

Any Energy Reducing improvement qualifies for this special rate. Everything from storm windows to roofing to hot water heaters. We want you to save money in energy cost, *now*.

You'll find there are many good reasons to talk to the loan officer at your local branch about saving money while saving energy.

Cordially,

YOUR SAVINGS INVESTED IN REAL ESTATE MORTGAGES LETTER

LETTER B-44

A successful cross-selling of banking services increased the real estate mortgage portfolio by 38 percent, for a small bank with under 20 million in assets.

Dear Saver:

Introducing . . .
the friendliest Real Estate Department on the mountain.

You have long been one of our passbook savings account holders. Did you ever wonder what your bank did with your savings? Someone just asked that question last week. And we think the answer was worth telling you, too.

First, your savings are insured by the F.D.I.C.

Second, your savings are invested, in part, in real estate mortgages to our neighbors and friends in the area.

Finally, your savings are sometimes invested in a real estate mortgage to yourself and members of your family.

Since you are a bank saver, we want to encourage you to use any of our services, including our skilled Real Estate Department. Since we already know you, we hope you will consider the little bank on the mountain when you want real estate loans. We can do a little "extra" for you in service.

Cordially,

THE "HOME HUNTER" BANKING SERVICE LETTER

LETTER B-45

Strangers to a community are glad to get assistance in locating the right housing for their family. Over the years, the bank has added thousands of new personal accounts, including some business accounts because of their willingness to be of personal service to new community residents.

Dear _____:

Let us be the first to wish you a very cordial welcome to our area.

The enclosed "Home Hunter's" kit is being sent to you as a free personal service of our bank—to make the transition from your present residence to your new home in our area a little easier.

In addition to our community guide, a free subscription to the newspaper, and other valuable information in our kit, we are also offering to you the following additional *free* services:

Home/Apartment Selector—a free service to assist you in locating an apartment, home or condominium. Simply return the Residence Selector form, and we'll put you in touch with a member of the local Board of Realtors.

Family Transfer Center—call us *collect* at _____. We can give you specific information concerning schools, taxes, and almost any subject relating to the area.

Bank Transfer Service—a simple and cost-free transfer of your bank accounts to make it easier for your family to shop immediately in our area. Return the enclosed Bank Transfer Card in the enclosed postage-paid envelope.

Write, or call us *collect* at the Family Transfer Center if we can be of assistance in making your move to our area a little easier.

Very truly yours,

"SEVEN REASONS WHY YOU'LL PREFER BANK FINANCED REAL ESTATE" LETTER

LETTER B-46

A successful marketing letter that generated a 27 percent increase in loan volume over the past year.

Seven Reasons Why You'll Prefer ABC Bank for Real Estate Financing

Your loan is almost as important as your home for satisfaction and security. Monthly payments and loan fees are important items that we will fully explain in planning your mortgage loan.

The ABC Bank offers seven reasons for real estate financial services:

1. *Experienced guidance.*
   Depend on ABC Bank for sound answers to your home financing questions. How much house can you afford? What about taxes and property insurance? Do you get merchandise title?

2. *Cost will not rise during life of loan.*
   You are protected against any increase in interest rates with an ABC real estate loan.

3. *Convenience.*
Our automatic loan payment plan makes repayment easy and time-saving.

4. *Complete financing services.*
We offer a full range of lending plans: conventional, 90%, 95%, FHA, VA, construction, multiple-family, commercial, condominium, and property improvement loans.

5. *Good service.*
ABC Bank makes every effort to process every loan quickly and correctly.

6. *Personal contact.*
The staff of our real estate department is always available to answer any questions or serve your needs. We'll even help when you are ready to sell or buy additional property.

7. *Property improvement loans.*
You can finance a remodeling project or improve your property with a low interest, no down payment loan.

Doesn't it make sense to consider ABC Bank—first—after you have found a house that fits your needs? Call us or ask your real estate broker to call.

Cordially,

KEEPING INDUSTRY IN TOWN LETTER

LETTER B-47

A bank letter extending credit accommodations that eliminated the expected loss of an important industry to the city.

Dear Mr. _____:

The ABC Bank is deeply committed to the growth of the electronics industry. Stock market analysts confirm our conviction that the growth in industrial and commercial electronics, particularly in the computer field, will be substantial. Since your firm is strongly related to the manufacture of data communications equipment, we at ABC Bank want to provide the necessary financial accommodations needed for you to capitalize on the tremendous opportunity at your doorstep.

Of course, we are desirous that you maintain your new plant facilities within the metropolitan area. The Chamber of Commerce is already at work on your behalf securing the necessary tax abatements for the new plant site. Your dynamic management is a plus to the general growth of the city as well as the data communication industry.

In addition to providing favorable construction loans, we want to offer our total banking services. If we can be of further service, please call me.

Cordially,

WE JUST CLOSED ONE MILLION DOLLARS IN REAL ESTATE LETTER

LETTER B-48

An innovative marketing letter to promote additional real estate mortgage business.

Dear Real Estate Broker:

Congratulations!

I'm sure your bank account is smiling, too. Now I know why you made so many smiling trips to the bank.

Our Real Estate Department just informed me that during the past year you were personally responsible for over one million dollars in real estate sales that were financed through the ABC Bank. Knowing the continuous shopping for the best financial real estate market that you are required to do as a real estate agent, we are pleased that you recommended us to your clients.

Be assured, we will endeavor to continue providing you and your clients with the best possible financial service. Should you ever feel we fall short in this task, please call me personally.

With warmest regards,

President

REAL ESTATE MORTGAGE PROMOTION LETTER

LETTER B-49

This general letter, mailed to all the real estate brokers in the area, was instrumental in increasing the banks' real estate loan volume from 90 million to 135 million in one year.

Dear Real Estate Broker:

As we close another successful real estate lending year, we want to thank all of our real estate friends who made possible our 90 million dollar ending real estate loan volume.

During the past year we closed over 3,200 residential, construction and commercial real estate loans. Your confidence in recommending the ABC Bank for real estate financing is the biggest factor in this splendid performance.

During the coming year, we are offering our real estate customers a financial planning gift to be presented by our closing officer, imprinted with the bank name *and* the real estate firm name. As a special gift to you, our closing officer will have prepared an engraved set of business cards with the name of your sales agent who handled the transaction. Enough to distribute to your next 100 business clients.

We wish you a bright and prosperous real estate year ahead.

Cordially,

Executive Vice-President, Real Estate Department

REAL ESTATE DEVELOPER PROMOTION LETTER

LETTER B-50

This letter aided in bringing in new business of 2½ million dollars for the bank.

Dear Developer:

If you are planning a new development, shopping center or apartment complex; you may be interested in the latest statistical analysis prepared just for developers by the ABC Bank Real Estate Department.

The economic well-being of our area is supported by the economic strength we enjoy over other regions. Some of the principal factors revealed by our analysis define the availability and future plans for transportation, availability and cost of power sources, nearness to markets for area manufacturers, present tax incentives, and the latest real estate financing opportunity.

We think you will find this unique report useful for planning purposes. Simply call our real estate department for your personal copy. If we can assist you with the complex financial planning, don't hesitate to ask for ABC Bank's "FINANCIAL GUIDELINES FOR DEVELOPERS."

Cordially.

SELLING BANK-OWNED REAL ESTATE LETTER

LETTER B-51

An effective prospect marketing letter for real property.

Dear _____:

Thank you for your interest and inquiry concerning the property at _____ which is owned by the ABC Bank.

The real estate is situated in an excellent location, and has been a profitable investment that provides a cash flow of 27% of the gross income after deduction of operating expenses, taxes and insurance. Presently, there are no vacancies. All units are under lease. During the past five years, the vacancy factor averaged 3¼%.

The enclosed brochure presents all detailed data on this investment. After you have an opportunity to review these interesting facts and figures, please call us at _____ for further information or an inspection of the premises.

Cordially,

"DO YOU HAVE TIME?" TRUST LETTER

LETTER B-52

This innovative trust department marketing letter, sent to large balance savings and checking account holders, resulted in a 12 percent reply and accounted for an increase of 132 new trust accounts.

Dear _____:

DO YOU HAVE TIME?

That is—can you afford to overlook the many advantages and services the ABC Bank offers from the Trust Department?

Good planning of wills and trusts can provide substantial savings to you or to your beneficiaries. Also, professional management of property can assure financial security for your family.

To help you achieve financial security, the ABC Bank can work closely with your attorney, life underwriter and accountant.

Our Trust Department can serve as Executor, Trustee under Wills and Living Trusts, managing agent of investments, custodian of securities, and Trustee under a self-employed retirement plan.

ABC's corporated services include stock registrar, transfer agent, and Trustee under pension and profit-sharing plans.

Call our Trust Department today. Let's spend some time together so you can become acquainted with our friendly and competent Trust Officers.

Respectfully yours,

"YOU'RE SOMEONE SPECIAL" TRUST LETTER

LETTER B-53

A unique approach to the cross-selling of banking services which creates a different marketing approach for the Trust Division.

Dear Bank Customer:

You're someone special to us at the ABC Bank!

Yes, as a checking or savings account customer you are very special to us. Special people are friends—those whom we try to please with our best performance. You are probably aware of the many services we have developed over the years just for friends—personal loans, safe deposit boxes and home mortgages. But have you thought about trust or estate planning for you or your family?

As the largest financial institution in the valley, ABC Bank offers the largest and most complete TRUST SERVICES just for special people like you. Our trust specialists can help you manage your money. Our trust officers will even work with your attorney to plan your estate.

If you have given any thought to trust or estate planning, please call us at _____. There is no obligation for a confidential discussion of this very special subject.

Cordially,

INVESTMENT PORTFOLIO PROMOTION LETTER

LETTER B-54

Selling the awareness of investment banking services.

Dear _____:

Today, the United States is generating goods and services at magical rates. Our Trust Department can show you how this tremendous economic growth will generate further growth and increase your personal opportunity for investment.

The improved profit prospects for corporations should attract renewed flow of foreign funds into the securities markets. This internationalization of investment holds a promise of improving the world's material standard of living. We at ABC Bank, have considerable data available that will help investors become aware of investment opportunities in this country. Also, we can provide specific information for direct investors as well as trust portfolio investors.

Our portfolio managers will be happy to discuss with you the investment aspects of the growth in primary metals, paper products, and the nearly overlooked 40% growth in foreign manufacturers entering U.S. manufacturing, during the past decade.

Call us for further information. Our Trust Department is ready to assist in your investment planning for increased earnings.

Cordially,

OFFERING TRUST AND INVESTMENT SERVICES LETTER

LETTER B-55

An introductory marketing letter, which replies to an inquiry about the bank's trust and investment services.

Dear _____:

We are pleased you inquired about our trust and investment banking services.

By working together, we can help you reach your long-range objectives. Only *you* know the needs and wants of you and your family. That is why we have many varied plans to help you and your family get more out of your investments—now—and in the years to come.

It would be best to arrange an appointment so we can discuss specifically how you can gain from our services. Won't you call me so we can plan a time to discuss your personal situation? In confidence, of course, without obligation.

Cordially,

RETIREMENT BENEFITS IN TRUST DEPARTMENT LETTER

LETTER B-56

Marketing a unique trust service to selected bank customers.

Dear Customer:

For over 35 years, the ABC Bank has provided skilled management in Trust Services. Now, the bank has approximately $180 million in trust assets including Pension, Profit-sharing, and Thrift plans.

Perhaps our Trust Service is another banking function you may want to explore for your benefit. Today, many salaried people are providing for retirement benefits to be paid into TRUST should they die before reaching age 65. By doing so, these retirement benefits retain whatever favorable tax treatment they would receive if paid to an individual beneficiary.

Perhaps now is the time to consider the advantages of having your retirement benefits administered by the ABC Bank as your trustee. Contact your attorney and then call us. Put us to work for you and your family.

Cordially,

Trust Department

"FREE FROM WORRY" TRUST SERVICES LETTER

LETTER B-57

Marketing trust services by cross-selling from the real estate and savings customers of the bank.

Dear Customer:

Have you considered the services offered by Our Trust Department?

If not, as a friend and customer of the ABC Bank you are familiar with the real estate banking service as well as our savings plans. It is our desire to introduce you to our Trust Department.

Our skilled technicians in the Trust Department can provide many services designed for your special requirements. Our Trust Department can provide day-by-day management of your real estate and other investments so you can be free from the worry of the details.

Our trust services can provide long range benefits, also. For example, an ABC Bank Timed Trust Plan for one family, saved in Federal Estate taxes over $51,400 on an asset valuation of $431,000. Estate tax planning is just one of the items our present bank customers should consider.

Talk to your attorney or call us at _____ so we may discuss the benefits of trust planning for you.

Cordially,

Trust Department

BUSINESS BUY-SELL TRUST AGREEMENT LETTER

LETTER B-58

Business account customers may need the additional banking service of the Buy-Sell impartial trustee plan.

Dear Customer:

We appreciate your choosing the ABC Bank as your business banking depository.

All the services of the bank are at your disposal including our trust services. So many business partnerships are concerned with the problems that can arise if one of the partners expires. The solution for some is a business buy-and-sell agreement life insurance policy. This allows the survivor to purchase the remaining business interest from the deceased partner's estate, and in a few situations allows the business to continue. As a service to our business customers we are prepared to act as impartial trustee, holding the insurance policies in trust.

Should your business be considering the establishment of the buy-and-sell insurance plan, we will be pleased to place our Trust Department at your disposal to administer the plan. Simply call us for an appointment.

Cordially,

Trust Department

ENERGY SOURCE INVESTMENT MARKETING LETTER

LETTER B-59

A unique letter stressing the expert skill of the bank in the energy source investment area. This letter can gain investor confidence in the portfolio management of the bank.

Dear Mr. and Mrs. —————:

Your request for investment management is an exciting challenge to me, personally. As I mentioned earlier, I presently manage several highly successful investment portfolios through the ABC Bank Trust Department.

Currently, I have been analyzing the demand for energy and have developed a future demand profile for the energy markets. With the use of our superior computer programs, we are able to pinpoint the major influences of the future rate of energy consumption.

When we look to the future, it appears from our computer research that energy consumption will require an increase of over 50% in energy sources. Our present data indicate coal consumption will double as will natural gas and water power energy consumption during the next decade. This means the locating of new energy sources will continue to be a number one priority. For example, nuclear power which was non-existent a few years ago can provide 15% of the country's energy in the 1980's.

If you would stop by the bank, I will be pleased to give you a detailed analysis of my projections in this area of investment opportunity. Also, I would like to show you several other exciting potential investments that the Trust Department is monitoring.

Sincerely,

"SAVE THE FAMILY FARM" TRUST PROMOTION LETTER

LETTER B-60

Unique marketing of trust services with a mailing to farm owners in the farm belt.

Dear —————:

As a customer of the ABC Bank, you may want to meet our newest Trust Officer.

Recently, Mr. ————— has joined us as Vice-President of Trust Services. His 15 years in banking Trust Services are now available to you for consultation of the most complex estates.

As you know, when an estate is transferred to the beneficiary, the problem of estate taxes must be settled. Some of our large area farms had to be broken up because of the tax situation that eliminated the long family tradition of farm ownership. Since estate taxes are graduated, two smaller estates pay less than one large estate. The net saving can amount to 32% or even 50% in the tax obligation when a farm passes from husband to wife and then to children.

Regardless of whether you own a large farm or a small house, call Mr. _____ so he can discuss confidentially how ABC banking Trust services can benefit you.

Cordially,

FOLLOW-UP TO CUSTOMER VISIT LETTER

LETTER B-61

A partial letter of thanks for a customer visit that shows personal interest in the bank customer.

The ABC Bank is in the unique position of being able to furnish your corporation with banking services best suited to your financial needs. We appreciate the opportunity to discuss your banking needs and offer services tailored to your specific requirements.

SHORT-TERM COMMERCIAL LOAN SERVICE LETTER

LETTER B-62

A partial letter to market the desirable commercial short-term loan.

We are pleased to extend the services of our Commercial Department to your business. Our 90-day working funds loan service offers you a stable financial program as you enter the heavy selling season. Adequate temporary working capital is a unique service that the ABC Bank can provide area retailers.

SPRINGTIME PROPERTY IMPROVEMENT MARKETING LETTER

LETTER B-63

A partial letter that sells the springtime do-it-now property improvement financing.

Spring is in the air. All things bright and beautiful is the theme for springtime.

Now is the time to start the important repair on your property. Redecorating offices and shops do so much to invite customers to step inside with a positive buying mood.

Won't you take a tip from Lady Springtime and put a new sparkle on those dormant repair plans? Your bank is ready to offer loan assistance for your repair and redecorating projects.

DEMAND DEPOSITS MARKETING LETTER

LETTER B-64

A partial letter to encourage increased demand deposits for the bank.

The lowest price in town—that is correct—we offer the package of six banking services at the lowest price in town for our checking account customers.

You receive free personalized checks, 10% rebate on installment loan finance charges, free traveler's checks, checking account overdraft protection, automatic checking-to-savings transfer, and 24-hour banking service.

We invite you to stop in at any branch of the ABC Bank to find out why the ABC Bank should be your banker.

CREDIT POINT-SCORING CONSUMER LOAN MARKETING LETTER

LETTER B-65

A partial letter that allows the customer to determine his own loan acceptance status.

Simply complete the enclosed point-score credit application. Follow the instructions on the bottom of the application and add up your own credit score. The ABC Bank has taken the mystery out of consumer credit approval. Now you can determine for yourself what your exact credit status is. Further, you will know in advance that you can be approved for your loan based on the total credit point-score that has been adopted by the bank.

We think that applying for a loan should be enjoyable—not a worry. Once you have completed the application, you can be your own credit approver. Send the application to the bank so we may check for accuracy, then sit back and wait for our "Yes."

GROUP *C* LETTERS

Fifteen Banking Goodwill Letters That Maximize Image

The Group C letters are the basic goodwill ambassadors of banking. The banker should plan to use these goodwill communicators to maximize the image of the bank. The letters in this group are friendly, warm and unexpected to the receiver. That is why they are so important to banking. The effects of these letters may develop months or even years later. These letters are excellent in long-range bank promotion, since they contain no direct marketing message.

The banking goodwill letter is generally favorably received and comes as an unexpected surprise. The human touch is apparent in this group of letters that show appreciation, offer special non-banking benefits, and congratulate someone for special achievements. The secret of this group is timing. Write promptly after learning about the event or the good news. The letters in this series offer time-saving promptness for the banker.

APPRECIATION OF MAYOR'S PROCLAMATION LETTER
LETTER C-1

Increase goodwill by showing appreciation to public officials.

Dear Mayor:

We at ABC Bank appreciate your proclamation of May 5, 19____, as "Radio Day."

Within the past two years this educational, non-profit radio program has increased the listening audience to approximately 20,000 avid fans at peak air times. The goal of the program is to serve the community.

It is the commendable support of leaders such as you, Mayor _____, that make educational programs a reality. Your continued support of this fine endeavor is greatly appreciated.

Yours for educational broadcasting,

ABC Bank

CHRISTMAS GOODWILL LETTER

LETTER C-2

There is little excuse for omitting the seasonal goodwill letters. They are read and convey your banking attitude.

Dear Mr. _____:

Christmas means many things, but at the ABC Bank the Holiday Season centers chiefly around the two finest things in life . . . Home and Friends.

Thinking of past Christmas Seasons makes us realize just how empty life would be without good friends.

So at this time of the year, we are thinking of you and how your friendship has been rewarding through the years. We hope you and your family will have a truly Merry Christmas and that the New Year will bring all your dreams come true for the good things in life.

Sincerely,

CONGRATULATIONS TO A NEW COMPANY OFFICER LETTER

LETTER C-3

Success provides a natural opportunity for goodwill boosting.

Dear _____ :

The morning paper carries a fine notice that you have been elected a Senior Vice-President of your company.

Congratulations!
It's a wise company you work for . . . they can pick talent and skill. I have no doubts about your future success.
Have a nice day!

Sincerely,

GOODWILL FOLLOWING THE FIRE LETTER

LETTER C-4

Unforeseen disasters can take their toll in the business world. A kind word is always welcome.

Dear Mr. _____ :

When I heard about the disastrous fire at your business, I was concerned about your well-being. After a hurried telephone call, I was relieved that neither you nor anyone else was injured in the blaze.

I can understand what a terrible loss this is to you at this time. But I am sure your company, under your leadership, will be back in business again.

If there is anything we at the bank can do to lessen your problems during the difficult rebuilding phase, just give me a call.

Yours truly,

STORE GRAND OPENING CONGRATULATIONS LETTER

LETTER C-5

Goodwill from the Branch Office.

Dear _____ :

Congratulations on the opening of your new store in the Town Mall.

You can rest assured I will be one of your customers, since my branch office is in the same shopping center. You'll like the atmosphere in the Town Mall and the variety of services for all of us working folks.

Whenever you're in the Town Mall ABC Bank Branch, I do hope you will stop by and visit with me. Whether for business or personal banking needs, I look forward to personally welcoming you to the Town Mall.

Sincerely,

Branch Manager

OFFER TO SOLVE BANKING PROBLEM LETTER

LETTER C-6

A unique letter that builds the bank's image while following-up on a customer inquiry.

Dear _____ :

Today we solved banking problems for two corporation presidents, a franchise owner, an independent grocer and a newspaper boy. But we missed seeing you today.

You probably thought that bankers are too busy to notice that you have not replied to our invitation to stop by for further discussion of your inquiry.

We want to be of service to you. Our bank has served the area for generations, taking an interest in the banking requirements of all our customers. We offer over thirty-eight unique services; one of which is tailored to solve your banking problem.

So do not hesitate to call us, no obligation of course, and we can aid in the solution to your banking problem.

Cordially,

INSURÁNCE BENEFIT FOR BANKING COMMUNITY LETTER

LETTER C-7

A special goodwill letter that maximizes the bank service image.

Dear Neighbor:

We are pleased to announce that we have completed arrangements with the Life Insurance Corporation, which will enable you and the members of your family to enroll in the "Guaranteed Issue Life Insurance Plan."

This is a unique Life Insurance Plan which makes it possible for you and your family to obtain an individual twenty-one payment life program, available to anyone from age 0 to 75 without medical examination. A licensed representative of Life Insurance Corporation will call on you in the near future to explain the details of the plan and answer any questions you may have.

As an added convenience to you, we have agreed to deduct the premium monthly from your account. In addition, Life Insurance Corporation has agreed to waive the handling charges which are customary when insurance premiums are paid other than yearly in advance.

Whether or not you wish to take advantage of this opportunity to enroll yourself and your family in this program is entirely your decision. We do feel, however, that this is an excellent way to add to your family's financial security.

Sincerely,

APPRECIATION OF BANK TOUR LETTER

LETTER C-8

A goodwill letter from one banker to another.

Dear _____:

Many thanks for your valuable time.

The tour and instructive information of your recent computerized data bank certainly gave us an insight into forward planning of banking projects.

Perhaps at some time I may reciprocate.

Sincerely,

APPRECIATION OF MANUFACTURING FACILITIES LETTER

LETTER C-9

A letter to all major manufacturers—customers and noncustomers—in the bank's service area.

Dear Manufacturer:

The past year was an exciting one for all of us. Starting the new year with a strong local economy is due in no small part to your business efforts.

We at the bank join with each family in the community in telling you that we are proud that you are part of the community team. Certainly, we wish next year will be even more prosperous for your company. Since many of your employees are banking customers, we are able to realize the close bond of association we all have throughout the community. Each of us is dependent on another for success.

We want to thank you for your continued support of the community and wish you a prosperous New Year.

Cordially,

HUMAN INTEREST IN BANKING LETTER

LETTER C-10

A letter that attracts attention to a unique human interest story that gives the bank a warm personality.

Dear _____:

We were so happy your Sixth Grade Class visited our bank last week. Your letter was very thoughtful.

Did you notice the painting on the lobby wall picturing a child who dropped the piggy bank outside the bank and a teller running to the child's rescue? The painting has an unusual story. The incident actually happened. The little girl grew into a young lady and an ardent bank customer. Remembering her childhood experience, the young lady painted the picture as a surprise gift to the bank. Today, the young lady is a successful artist and associate professor at the University.

Of course, we are very proud of the youth of our community. You and your class are always welcome to visit the bank, anytime.

Yours very truly,

THE AMERICAN DREAM SUCCESS LETTER

LETTER C-11

A letter of congratulations to individuals listed in various media as going into business for themselves.

Dear _____:

Your announcement in the newspaper concerning the start of
your own business was well received by the business community. We want to extend best wishes to you for a successful
future.

You are not alone in your desire to own a business. One of the
greatest of all American Dreams is for most men to one day
operate their own business. We are fortunate in America to
have this unique privilege—the right to own property and to
own a business.

It is just such people as you who have made this a strong
community. We are proud to welcome you to the growing ranks
of business owners.

Cordially,

THE GOODWILL BENEFIT OF LOCAL BRANCH BANKING LETTER

LETTER C-12

A partial letter that maximizes the banking image by explaining the
customer benefits of branch banking.

One of the reasons so many banking customers are enthusiastic over the local branch banking program is the special individual service they received by banking locally. This is why we
are dedicated to the branch banking program. We intend to
bring banking services to our customers at convenient locations near home or work.

SEASON'S GREETINGS GOODWILL LETTER

LETTER C-13

A partial letter to convey friendship at Christmas time.

The Holiday Season gives us an opportunity to express our
friendship. In this spirit and with kind thoughts of the year-long
business relationship that we have shared, we wish you the
best of health and good fortune during the New Year.

"THANK YOU" TO A SPEAKER LETTER

LETTER C-14

A partial letter to thank a business speaker in a gracious manner.

The record attendance for our meeting shows the great interest in your topic. To be sure, your personal reputation as a speaker and national authority was the significant reason for our overflow attendance. Many of our members asked if you will be available for another lecture soon. If you will give me your future speaking dates, I will publish them in our newsletter. Many of our members will want to attend other lectures concerning your dynamic topic.

"THANK YOU" FOR A COMPLIMENTARY LETTER

LETTER C-15

A partial letter to thank a customer for her complimentary letter.

Seldom does anyone take the time to tell another about a pleasant business transaction. So when your letter arrived, I was deeply flattered that you wrote. The comments in your letter will be read to our bank staff, as they demonstrate that someone really does care about the friendly smiles and pleasant service that every business should require as normal business practice.

We will always strive to earn your respect by extending friendly and pleasant banking service.

GROUP *D* LETTERS

Twenty Letters That Solve the Communications Problem for Trust and Estate Situations

Trust and investment services are people-oriented banking services. This unit of the bank is designed to enable customers to gain more income and security from their assets.

No two situations or customers have identical needs in trust and investment services. For that reason, the bank's professional trust department is a valuable part of banking. Also, it is uniquely different from other banking services. The group D letters provide twenty different letters that solve the broad spectrum of the complicated communications required by trust and investment portfolio bankers.

Managing the investments in trust for another requires special communications to insure that needed confidence. Settling an estate has special problems: handling estate taxes, explaining the function of trust accounts, or informing the customer about investment goals that work are unique communications problems that can require many hours—even days—to correctly reduce into writing. This series provides ready-to-use letters that allow more time for managing the funds instead of explaining how we manage the funds.

SETTLING THE ESTATE LETTER

LETTER D-1

A difficult and delicate situation requiring the best explanation from the bank's Trust Department.

Dear Mr. _____ :

As executor for your father's estate, we take the business of settling the estate very seriously. As we knew your father personally, we at the ABC Bank are saddened by his untimely passing.

Briefly, to answer the many questions you may have, we act for you and the other beneficiaries in the following manner:

- we gather all the assets together
- we determine if there are any unpaid bills or if anyone owes money to the estate; including continuing royalties
- we set aside necessary reserves to pay taxes, debts and other expenses
- we will analyze the long-term value of securities to be held either by you and the other beneficiaries, or managed in trust
- we will determine the estate's tax obligation under the various options available to the executor
- we will compute and file the final tax returns as required

All of our records concerning your father's estate are open to review by you and other beneficiaries for your approval of the accuracy of our estate decisions. I look forward to an opportunity to meet with you for a review of the estate.

Cordially,

Trust Department

INVESTMENTS IN A RETIREMENT FUND LETTER

LETTER D-2

A skilled letter that adds to the professionalism of the Trust Department.

Dear Mr. _____:

Your retirement fund investments are in skilled hands with ABC Bank Trust Management.

Meeting your goals and objectives is the investment policy prescribed by our Trust Officers. Our stated policy in common stock for fixed income management requires that we invest in corporations that meet the following criteria:

- Prominent industry position
- Strong financial position and adequate marketability
- Long-term demand for the company products
- Solid quality and depth of management
- Total return expectation at 1½ times long-term bond rates
- Regular dividend payments

Our policy for bonds requires a rating of A or better by Standard & Poor, and Moody's. Also, we maintain a safe ratio between stocks and bonds. The portfolio is approved by you and our Trust Department prior to implementation. Jointly, we establish a management benchmark for the monitoring of our investment performance.

Our experienced staff of portfolio managers stand ready to be responsive to your administrative and investment needs.

Cordially,

MEET THE PORTFOLIO OR INVESTMENT
TRUST MANAGER LETTER

LETTER D-3

Strong support for the skills of top-notch portfolio managers is emphasized in this letter.

Dear Mr. _____:

In response to your request for information concerning the handling of your trust investments, we want to assure you that ABC Bank relies on the skilled expertise of staff professionals in our Trust Department.

The total department is supported with rapid computer information, interpretation and communication to the trust portfolio manager. Each customer account is assigned a portfolio manager who is personally responsible for the daily operations in their respective areas.

Your portfolio manager has responsibility for management of the common stock segment and the coordination of all asset segments of the portfolio. The daily management of your non-common stock segments, such as your bonds, oil leases and real estate; is assigned to specialists for each of the particular assets.

We are able to rapidly analyze the daily fluctuations in your total trust account and act immediately for your benefit according to your guidelines. Any time you want to discuss a unique situation with our trust specialists, please call on us.

Cordially,

ESTATE TAXES IN TRUST SITUATIONS

LETTER D-4

A response to the beneficiary of the living trust inquiring about ownership and taxation.

Dear Mrs. _____:

Thank you for your inquiry about your parents' lifetime trust. You have my condolences on the passing of your mother, who will be remembered as one of the city's leading citizens.

Briefly, the trust plan with the bank that had been established by your parents did allow them both to be free of the management worries. Following your father's death, the income from the securities continued during your mother's lifetime. The actual securities go to you and your three brothers, now that your mother has passed away.

Under provisions of the trust, your mother never owned the securities for tax purposes. Therefore, her estate will pay no tax on these securities. You and your brothers benefit from the nontaxable transfer of the securities.

Your attorney, of course, will be aware of the details of the trust program. However, we will be glad to assist in any manner we can. Please call me whenever I can be of service.

Sincerely,

TRUST SERVICES LETTER

LETTER D-5

A promotional letter that added additional trust accounts for the bank.

Dear Mr. _____:

Whatever your financial needs—think of ABC Bank.

Our Trust Department can provide management of your securities and property, and perhaps provide savings in costs; including taxes.

We have a staff of investment experts that are willing to go to work immediately for you. Tell us your investment objectives when you open your account, and then we'll take the best action possible to keep your portfolio working toward your personal goals.

All securities are under daily review. If charges are necessary, we are in a position to act for you immediately. Our annual tax statement can help in the preparation of your income tax return.

If you want to discuss your portfolio and our management services, we will be glad to talk to you at a time convenient to you.

Cordially,

EMPLOYEE BENEFIT TRUST LETTER

LETTER D-6

A useful letter that brings in co-mingled equity funds and co-mingled fixed funds.

Dear _____:

Recently, we replied to your request for information on a proposal involving the management of employee benefit assets by _____ Bank.

Now that you have had the opportunity to review our proposal, we will be happy to offer any additional information you may desire. We have updated the Co-mingled Equity Funds to February 28, 19___ and added Co-mingled Fixed Funds as of February 28, 19___ to our proposal.

If you would like to receive this new information, please contact us and we will be happy to send it to you.

If you would like to personally discuss this proposal further, please write me; or call me collect at _____. I will look forward to hearing from you and stand ready to respond to your inquiry.

Sincerely,

Vice President and Trust Officer

ADMINISTERING THE TRUST LETTER
LETTER D-7

Sell the benefits of trust administration.

Dear Mr. _____:

Thank you for an opportunity to administer your trust.

As we mentioned, our function is to serve you now and your beneficiaries later. As trustee, we will put our investment skills to work for you. In the event of illness or other emergency, your beneficiaries can be confident that we are continuously working for their financial security. We will pay all medical and household bills directly from the trust until the beneficiary is recovered and able to assume control again; regardless of any change of residence.

We stand ready to serve you and your beneficiary at any time, any place. Of course, should any questions arise, call me at once.

Sincerely,

Trust Department

MANAGING EMPLOYEE BENEFITS LETTER
LETTER D-8

A profitable letter used to gain new trust business.

Dear Mr. _____:

Enclosed is a proposal concerning the Management of Employee Benefit Assets by our bank's Trust Department.

You will notice in the proposal, we have not discussed bond portfolios or short-term cash management. This is because most of our customers are interested in results related to equities management. We are, however, happy to provide you with fixed income management schedules if desired.

Our current philosophy for portfolio mixes with no actual direction or instruction from you would require a 10% to 20% cash position (opportunity money), with the remaining portfolio invested 60% bonds and 40% stocks. Of course, your input will be the determining factor tempered by the economic outlook.

The proposal is complete, but if you wish additional information do not hesitate to contact us.

Sincerely,

Trust Officer

PORTFOLIO SAFETY IN A TRUST ACCOUNT LETTER

LETTER D-9

In response to a typical inquiry about the safety of the stocks and bonds in a trust account.

Dear _____:

Your concern for the safety of the trust portfolio is shared by us at ABC Bank.

As you know, the securities markets are regulated both by the governmental authorities and by the security industry. Federal legislation covers investor activities, new security issues, and publicly held investment companies. Much of this legislation compels corporate disclosure information which the ABC Bank trust officers read and analyze carefully.

For example, to protect investors, the New York Stock Exchange has minimum size requirements for companies whose shares it lists. These are a few of the minimum requirements:

- earn $2.5 million before taxes in the previous year
- hold $14 million of net tangible assets
- possess $14 million in market value of publicly held common stock
- have publicly held 800,000 common shares of each million shares outstanding

Of course, we feel that the specialized analysis of your portfolio by the trust officer is our way of protecting your investment. Please feel free to call us to discuss any situation that should arise involving your trust account.

Cordially,

REVOCABLE LIFETIME TRUST BENEFITS LETTER

LETTER D-10

Why establish the trust account? Several beneficial reasons are explored successfully.

Dear Mr. _____:

The successful management of your investments in the complex rise and fall of today's markets requires considerable time in order to watch developments affecting your investments.

For most of us, there are simply not enough hours in the day to handle the more important things to be done and to constantly watch developments affecting our securities, such as:

- acting on stock rights or tender offers
- investment news that affects the portfolio
- new investment opportunities that are announced

It is possible through our Trust Department, to create a revocable lifetime trust and eliminate the worries about lack of time with us on the job looking after your securities as trustee.

We'll be happy to supply, without obligation on your part, more information on a lifetime trust. Call us for an appointment so we may discuss with you the full advantages of the revocable living trust.

Cordially,

TRUST SERVICES—PENSION ADMINISTRATION LETTER

LETTER D-11

A starting point for designing the investment program for a pension plan of a company.

Dear Mr. _____:

Thank you for your inquiry.

ABC Bank has one of the more experienced staffs of pension administration specialists in the country. We take pride in our experience and capacity to handle nearly all recordkeeping requirements. Our Trust Services Department has its own computer and recordkeeping program which ensures accurate and timely reports.

ABC Bank will design an investment program to meet your specific goals. The portfolio managers are trained to coordinate conservative ABC banking philosophy with the objectives of your fund. Our superior record of common stock management is a result of our clear and consistent investment philosophy combined with a very capable staff of portfolio managers.

The initial meeting with an investment officer can be established at your convenience to determine your investment objectives and the special requirement of your program. We look forward to being of service to you.

Cordially,

Trust Officer

EXPLAINING THE EMPLOYEE RETIREMENT INCOME SECURITY ACT OF 1974 LETTER

LETTER D-12

An informational letter for the company responsible for employee retirement programs.

Dear Customer:

We want to pass along some important information concerning Employee Benefit Plans.

The passage of the Employees Retirement Income Security Act of 1974 brings with it additional concern about the potential liability and responsibility in the administration of Employee Benefit Plans. The act provides that any Fiduciary who breaches any requirements is personally liable for any losses to the plan.

Under the Act, a fiduciary is required to:

- discharge his duties solely in the interest of plan participants and beneficiaries for the exclusive purpose of providing plan benefits to them and defraying the reasonable expenses of administering the plan.
- act with care and skill using the prudent man concept in the conduct of the plan.
- diversify plan investments to minimize risk of large losses unless it is clearly not prudent to diversify.
- operate in accordance with plan instruments and documents.
- not enter into certain activities and transactions.

The Employee Benefit Participants must now be automatically furnished with a summary of the annual report reflecting information about the plan and investment transactions.

As a new customer of our trust services, we are happy to keep you abreast of current requirements in administration of your Employee Benefit Plan Should you have any questions, please feel free to call us.

Cordially,

"WHY THE LIFE INSURANCE TRUST?" LETTER

LETTER D-13

A letter to selected bank customers that adds a new dimension of banking service.

Dear Mr. _____:

You purchased life insurance for protection. Will your family really enjoy the total benefit of your insurance program?

The methods by which your insurance benefits are paid are of vital importance to your beneficiaries:

- should you leave your proceeds outright?
- should you leave the proceeds under a "settlement option"; a feature offered by the insurance firm?
- should you establish a life insurance trust through the ABC Bank Trust Department?

As simple as life insurance seems—all you need to do is PAY premiums—it is more complex if you want to be assured of the maximum benefits for your family. We will help you determine which plan is most favorable for you and your family. Call us so we can help in planning a better future.

Cordially,

REVOCABLE LIFE INSURANCE TRUST

LETTER D-14

Acknowledgment of the trust agreement that answers some common questions.

Dear Mr. _____:

Yes, the Life Insurance Trust Agreement drawn by your attorney is revocable and subject to change at any time during your lifetime.

Under the trust agreement, the proceeds of the life insurance policies are to be invested by our Trust Department and the income to be paid to your wife during her lifetime. As you stipulated, should your wife become ill and unable to sign checks, for example, we will handle these items directly from the trust.

You have instructed us in the agreement to divide the property equally among the children when your wife passes away. At that point the trust is to end. However, if you should decide on changing the final distribution of the trust agreement, it can be done. You can still borrow on the insurance policies or even surrender them for the cash value if you so desire.

We are pleased to assist in any planning aspects. Do not hesitate to call me if I can be of help.

Sincerely,

Trust Department

TRUSTEED PROFIT-SHARING PLAN LETTER

LETTER D-15

This letter, sent to selected bank customers with strong assets, accounted for twenty-seven new trust accounts.

Dear Mr. _____:

You should enjoy your leisure years without financial worry.

After all your years of hard work, you should plan your time to enjoy yourself. Upon receiving your benefits from the company Trusteed Profit-Sharing Plan, why not turn it over to us as your trustees? We are prepared to handle the work and worry of investing the funds for you.

Call us for an appointment so we can explain how we can put your profit-sharing money to work for you, while you plan that long-dreamed of vacation cruise or fishing trip.

Cordially,

Trust Department

MARKETING REAL ESTATE LEASE IN TRUST LETTER

LETTER D-16

The following letter was used to fill four vacant office spaces in an office building held by the bank's trust management department. The space was filled in three weeks.

Dear Real Estate Broker:

Among your clients you may have a professional group that requires prestigious office space. An office that will enhance the group's image, contacts and possible earnings.

We have four vacant spaces in one of our buildings managed by our bank's Trust Department. The _____ Building offers excellent facilities and services combined with ideal location; perfect for people who need a location that reflects the dignity and professionalism of their workstyle.

The _____ Building offers security guards, accessable parking, air-conditioned luxury suites and maintenance personnel on duty during business hours.

And there's more . . . our professional interior designers and decorators will create an office for the specific needs of your professional group. We always custom-design each suite to fit the particular needs of your client.

For you, consider this as a co-op real estate transaction. Yes, the commission would be based on the entire term of the lease.

Please call me for further information.

Sincerely,

Trust Department

BALANCING LONG-TERM VS. SHORT-TERM
INVESTMENT GOALS LETTER

LETTER D-17

The stressing of objectives assures better trust and investment customer relations.

Dear Customer:

In our effort to keep trust clients informed of our investment objectives, we want to state ABC Bank's guidelines.

We balance your long-term vs. short-term priority of achieving an investment goal. We plan for your required rate of return as defined by you. Of course, we consider the interplay of the present size of the investment, the estimated size and timing of future contributions, and the estimated goals during the next five years.

Also, the suitability of using higher risk segments of stocks is considered carefully. In addition, the application and composition of royalty, mineral, and real estate investments in the investment trust is reviewed in line with your defined trust and investment program.

If at any time, you would like an in-depth review of the portfolio, please call us.

Cordially,

"HOW ARE WE DOING?" THE TRUST ANSWER LETTER

LETTER D-18

When the beneficiary or individual inquires about performance, the bank sends this performance winner.

Dear _____:

Thank you for your inquiry into the investment portfolio.

We are pleased to give you a performance benchmark enabling you to judge your trust portfolio with ABC Bank. When we review the annual rates of return on the common stock performance, we can compare the Standard and Poor's 500, which reflected a 3.2% compound annual rate of return for the cumulative period of five years 19X1–19X5. Our total trust portfolios reflected a 3.74%. As you will note from the detailed analysis enclosed, your individual portfolio did better.

It is our objective to provide expert trust services commensurate with the directions and input from you. Should you have any further questions, please contact me.

Cordially,

Trust Department

"LESS CONTROVERSY UNDER TRUST PLAN" LETTER

LETTER D-19

In trust—we can keep your assets a secret.

Dear Mr. _____:

Yes, you are correct that wills can be under attack by disappointed heirs. Objections can be raised that a will is faulty because of a technicality in its wording resulting in unnecessary litigation.

The revocable trust, as we discussed, is effective throughout your lifetime. Any questions that arise about the wording of the trust agreement can be resolved by establishing any correction you desire; during your lifetime. The revocable trust gives you an opportunity to observe your estate plan in operation. Also, it is adaptable to your changing views and can be modified to suit your needs.

A trust is a private agreement, while a will is usually a matter of public record. The terms of a will can receive unwanted publicity, while the trust generally is not subject to public attention.

Should you have any further questions, I will be happy to answer them.

Cordially,

ABC Bank

THE TRUST ESTATE SERVICES LETTER
LETTER D-20

The little things that make a trust account so nice.

Dear Mr. _____:

While we are handling your trust agreement, we will be completely objective and reliable. The full resources of the bank stand behind all of our actions, so that your beneficiaries are protected at all times. Our management decisions are made with one thought in mind: to carry out your instructions in the best interest of your family.

Should you become disabled, we are prepared to watch your investments daily, deposit funds in your bank accounts, write checks and pay bills. You can devote all your time to regaining your health—without worry about your extensive investments. We will step in, when and if you need us.

We look forward to a long and pleasant relationship in working with you in the management of your trust account at ABC Bank.

Cordially,

GROUP *E* LETTERS

Thirty-seven Top-flight Bank Credit Letters to Handle All the Major Credit Situations

Credit has been responsible for many a business success and for the country's powerful production capacity. The banking system has made credit the future monetary basis. As banks evolve toward the electronic funds transfer systems, credit correspondence will be more extensive. Speed will be an absolute necessity in evaluating credit situations.

The Group E letters provide top-flight bank credit correspondence to support all the major credit situations. A major function of the bank is to distribute credit. With the rise of retail banking or consumer credit, banks need additional communication tools. These tools are included here—a letter to explain the Annual Percentage Rate, bank credit card letters, over the credit limit control letters, credit rejection letters, notice of right of rescission form letter as provided by the Board of Governors of the Federal Reserve System—also, the commercial credit letters that are required in our modern banking business are provided for improved credit control and response.

Bank credit properly handled tends to create a closer relationship between the bank and the customer. The device selected to communicate either a favorable or unfavorable credit decision will leave a lasting impression on the customer. Bad credit letters can result in the bank's communication being read into the Congressional Record, which actually happened to a poorly planned bank credit letter. As mundane as credit letters appear to be, the tone and message structure are important aspects of the credit letter.

"WHAT IS THE ANNUAL PERCENTAGE RATE?" LETTER

LETTER E-1

A top-flight explanation of a most difficult credit term.

Dear Mr. _____:

In response to your letter about the Annual Percentage Rate on your bank installment loan, we are pleased to be able to explain this terminology that is now required as a result of the Truth-In-Lending Act, Regulation Z.

The payments are applied first to interest due and any remainder is then applied to reduce principal. This is called the actuarial method. To illustrate, we will quote a simple example from the Board of Governors of the Federal Reserve System:

> A bank loan of $100 repayable in equal monthly installments over one year is made at a 6% add-on charge. The annual percentage rate would be 11%. The borrower would repay $106 over one year. He would only have use of the full $100 until he made his first payment, and less and less each month as payments are made. The effect is that the actual annual percentage rate is almost twice the add-on percentage rate.
>
> (Truth-In-Lending Regulation Z, amended to March 23, 1977)

This actuarial method is complicated and the Federal Reserve Board has prepared tables showing the various annual percentage rates. On your loan, the annual percentage rate is computed at ____%. This information was shown on your original loan processing papers. We hope this explanation of a complicated term answers your inquiry. However, if you need additional information, please call us.

Cordially,

EXPLAINING THE BANK CREDIT CARD
FINANCE CHARGE LETTER

LETTER E-2

Every bank offering or planning a bank card plan must expect to receive inquiries about the calculation of the finance charge. Establish a pre-printed form letter and solve a recurring customer inquiry.

Thank you for your inquiry and interest in our bank credit card plan. We will be happy to explain how the credit card finance charges are computed.

The finance charge is based on the ending balance of the previous month's statement. The finance charge becomes part of your new bank credit card balance.

The rate is computed at ____% per month on the previous balance up to $____ and the balance in excess is computed at ____% per month, with a minimum service charge of $.50 for any month with a carry-over unpaid balance. The annual percentage rate is ____%. Should you choose to remit the balance in full within 24 days of the billing date, no service charge is applied in that following month. We offer a flexible budget plan for your use and convenience by paying in full, eliminating service charges, or paying at least the minimum payment required. For your convenience, billing dates are clearly identified on your bank credit card statement.

We appreciate your shopping with the bank credit card. If we can make your use of the card more convenient, please contact us.

Cordially,

RESPONSE TO ANGRY BANK BORROWER LETTER

LETTER E-3

This letter averted a large lawsuit that was being initiated by a disgruntled bank customer.

Dear Mr. _____:

Thank you for your letter of _____ addressed to the Bank President. We appreciate your writing, thereby affording us an opportunity to investigate the circumstances you describe and take appropriate action.

Upon its receipt, we forwarded your letter to Mr. _____, Vice President of the Installment Loan Department. He assured us that it will be given prompt attention and that he will furnish you with a detailed explanation of the circumstances you mentioned. You can expect to hear further on this situation, shortly.

It is always a matter of concern to us when any customer feels that he is receiving unfair treatment and that he can no longer continue as a customer of the ABC Bank. Be assured, Mr. _____, that we value your business. Please accept our apologies for any inconvenience you may have been caused.

Very truly yours,

CORRESPONDENT BANK NEEDS INFORMATION LETTER

LETTER E-4

Building a chain of credit information sources.

Dear Mr. _____:

One of our correspondent banks has asked our assistance in obtaining information relative to the purchase of commercial notes from the _____ Corporation, at _____ street, (*city*).

It would be useful if you would supply a brief summary of your financial experience with the company. The corporation has indicated you are a primary lending source. Of course, all comments and information will be treated confidentially.

Our correspondent bank will be pleased to reciprocate at any time, as we have in the past.

Sincerely,

CREDIT INQUIRY ON COMMERCIAL NOTES LETTER

LETTER E-5

Credit history is vital to banking success.

Dear _____:

We are revising our credit information on the _____ Corporation. Under consideration is the purchase of their corporate notes. Therefore, we would appreciate receiving your comments about the management and financial stability of the company.

Also, we would appreciate revising your loan experience information, including the present line and high credit.

This information will be held in confidence and we will be happy to return your favor whenever you have need of similar information.

Sincerely,

OVER THE CREDIT LIMIT CUSTOMER LETTER

LETTER E-6

An effective notice that generally receives a payment response upwards of 20 percent from customers.

Date

Account No.

Balance

Amount overlimit

Dear Customer:

Thank you for your recent purchases on the ABC Bank Credit Card. Presently, your balance is higher than the approved credit limit of _____. Of course, this may be because of payments or credits not yet received.

However, if there are no offsetting credits or payments, please pay the amount of overlimit shown above *before* making any additional purchases. We want to make your shopping as **easy** and as pleasant as possible.

ABC Bank

NOTIFICATION OF NON-REISSUANCE OF
BANK CREDIT CARD LETTER

LETTER E-7

Used as a form credit information letter, it takes the sting out of suspended credit on reissue of a bank credit card.

Account No.

Dear Mr. _____:

IMPORTANT . . .

Your credit record indicates that your bank card is presently not available for *reissuance*.

Your account is in arrears or exceeds the authorized credit limit by _____. Just as soon as the situation is corrected, we would promptly like to send you your new bank card.

Please send this notice with your payment, so your bank card can be in the mail to you quickly.

ABC Bank

APPLICATION REJECTION LETTER

LETTER E-8

A bad news letter that allows the customer to save face.

Dear Customer:

We appreciate your application for an installment loan with the ABC Bank.

At this time, we are not able to comply with your request for the loan as requested. Many factors are considered in evaluating applications: job longevity, length of residency, income, net worth, ratio of income to liabilities, credit history and number of dependents.

As much as we regret to decline your application, we are compelled to do so if any of the requirements for approval are not present.

However, it has been our experience that individuals who do not meet our requirements today may be qualified at a later date. In your case, we do cordially invite you to re-apply at a later date.

Sincerely,

ABC Bank

CREDIT REFUSAL LETTER

LETTER E-9

Every customer must be notified of the reason for rejection.

Dear _____:

Thank you for your recent application for a bank loan.

Your request has been considered most carefully, but we regret that we are unable to grant the loan request at this time.

Perhaps in the future we can reconsider your request, if you want to re-apply at that time.

You may call us at _____ for an explanation of our decision, if you desire.

Sincerely,

REFUSAL OF LOAN APPLICATION LETTER

LETTER E-10

Maintain goodwill as you inform the customer of bad news.

Dear Mr. _____:

Our job at ABC Bank is to approve every loan possible. That's how we make money. Unfortunately, some loans must be refused. Generally, customers appreciate knowing the reason why.

After careful consideration of your loan request, we reluctantly are unable to grant your request at this time. Your present monthly obligations plus a payment on the new loan request will not leave a safe margin for emergencies.

Of course, we may be wrong. But we feel we can better serve you by suggesting a deferral of this new purchase until a time when your current obligations are reduced. At a later date we will certainly consider your request again.

Thank you for thinking of ABC Bank when you are interested in financing.

Cordially,

NOTICE OF RIGHT OF RESCISSION FORM LETTER

LETTER E-11

The following form is the notice of the right to rescind a transaction, required to be given to customers under certain circumstances set forth in Section 226.9 of Regulation Z. This information and form were furnished by The Board of Governors of the Federal Reserve System. *Further, the form must be set in 12 point boldface type as a minimum.*

(Identification of Transaction)

Notice to Customer Required by Federal Law:

You have entered into a transaction on (*date*) which may result in a lien, mortgage, or other security interest on your home. You have a legal right under Federal Law to cancel this transaction, if you desire to do so, without any penalty or obligation within three business days from the above date or any later date on which all material disclosures required under the Truth-In-Lending Act have been given to you. If you so cancel the transaction, any lien, mortgage, or other security interest on your home arising from this transaction is automatically void. You are also entitled to receive a refund of any downpayment or other consideration if you cancel. If you decide to cancel this transaction, you may do so by notifying

---

(*Name of Creditor*)

At _____

(*Address of Business*)

by mail or telegram sent not later than midnight of (*date*). You may also use any other form of written notice identifying the transaction if it is delivered to the above address not later than that time. This notice may be used for that purpose by dating and signing below.

I hereby cancel this transaction.

(*Customer's signature*)

Effect of Rescission. When a customer excercises his right to rescind under paragraph (a) of this section, he is not liable for any finance or other charge, and any security interest becomes void upon such a rescission. Within 10 days after receipt of a notice of rescission, the creditor shall return to the customer any money or property given as earnest money, downpayment, or otherwise, and shall take any action necessary or appropriate to reflect the termination of any security interest created under the transaction. If the creditor has delivered any property to the customer, the customer may retain possession of it. Upon the performance of the creditor's obligations under this section, the customer shall tender the property to the creditor, except that if return of the property in kind would be impracticable or inequitable, the customer shall tender its reasonable value. Tender shall be made at the location of the property or at the residence of the customer, at the option of the customer. If the creditor does not take possession of the property within 10 days after tender by the customer, ownership of the property vests in the customer without obligation on his part to pay for it.

INDORSING CUSTOMER CHECKS LETTER

LETTER E-12

An important explanation to a business as a banking service.

Dear Customer:

We want to clarify the explanation on the check returned against your account today.

As a merchant you should know the indorser. Your cashiers must be certain they can identify the person presenting the check to you. The indorsement of your customer makes it possible for you to require him to make payment if the check is dishonored.

In this case, the original payee has not indorsed the check. A notice has been placed on the payroll check that this check was lost. Therefore, the check for $242.38 cannot be presented for payment. We urge you to check with your indorser for recovery of your funds.

Cordially,

RETURNING A CONDITIONAL INDORSEMENT CHECK LETTER

LETTER E-13

The bank does not want to assume the responsibility of determining whether or not the condition has been met.

Dear Customer:

Regretfully, we must return the enclosed check which was included with your deposit of _____, 19____.

The check for $_____ dated _____ has a CONDITIONAL INDORSEMENT which authorizes payment under certain named conditions. For us to process this check would require additional liability upon the bank.

We suggest you contact your customer and secure a new check without the conditional indorsement.

Cordially,

APPROVED BANK CREDIT CARD CUSTOMER LETTER

LETTER E-14

Dear Customer:

Your ABC Bank Credit Card application was approved. We are happy to inform our over 3,000 merchants that honor ABC's Bank Card that you are on the growing list of newly approved cardholders.

Now your shopping will be more convenient, with more variety to choose from at special sales. You are also eligible for a cash advance, for any purpose, simply by presenting your ABC Card at any bank in the United States displaying the distinctive card emblem.

Thank you for another opportunity to serve your banking needs.

Sincerely,

LOAN APPROVAL LETTER

LETTER E-15

Explain the terms and tell the customer the loan is approved.

Dear _____:

Your application for a loan with ABC Bank has been approved. Thanks for thinking ABC when you decided on your financing.

As mentioned at the time you made the application, your payments are $_____, due in installments on the first of each month. For your information, the Annual Percentage Rate is ___%.

We look forward to being of service in any of your banking needs. If it is convenient, automatic transfers from your checking account are possible. Simply ask any teller for the authorization card.

Cordially,

INTRODUCING THE NEWEST CREDIT SERVICE LETTER

LETTER E-16

Combining marketing flavor with the notice of account approval.

Dear Valued Customer:

Welcome! Thank you for choosing _____, ABC Bank's newest service which opens the door to thousands upon thousands of stores, shops and service businesses not only in your area, but around the world.

You'll find that your new _____ card is safer and more convenient than making purchases with cash. However, when it comes to cash, your card is your "passport" to "instant loan" service at any of ABC's convenient branch locations or at any other bank, anywhere, displaying the _____ emblem. Money for holiday shopping, bill paying, or any other purpose—it's right there at your fingertips with your new red and gold card; the most valuable and most accepted bank card in the world.

_____ is another convenient ABC Bank service. Remember, our staff is waiting to welcome you and your red and gold "passport" to instant funds.

Best wishes for a Happy Holiday Season!

Sincerely,

President

APPRECIATION FOR A GOOD PAYMENT RECORD LETTER

LETTER E-17

A "thank you" for prompt payment of a recent loan encourages the better customers to use the loan services of your bank.

Dear Customer:

We wish to express our appreciation for the excellent manner in which you have handled your recent account at the ABC Bank. You are deserving of a very special thanks. As a result, we have enclosed your EXCELLENT CUSTOMER IDENTIFICATION CARD.

At any ABC Bank office, this card is instant identification and assures prompt service. Just show it to any installment loan counselor in any ABC Bank branch whenever you want to buy another automobile, make improvements on your home or consolidate your debts.

With this card, you may also receive a loan for vacations, furniture or any good reason. Your excellent record entitles you to special handling on your next loan with ABC Bank.

We want to see you receive the funds you need. So, do stop and see us soon.

Sincerely,

Vice President, Installment Loan Division

PAID AHEAD OF SCHEDULE LOAN LETTER

LETTER E-18

If all customers paid as agreed or ahead of schedule, our work would be easier.

Dear Customer:

Your final payment coupon just reached my office. It is always a pleasure to mark a loan file "Better than agreed." This notation was added to your customer record file.

If all our customers handled their obligations in the serious manner in which you normally do, banking would be more pleasant for us in the Loan Department. Your commendable payment record should be a source of pride to you. After all, sixty payments paid on time and five months early is a major responsibility. Now you can enjoy the home improvement without thinking about another payment.

Thank you for your prompt payments. Whenever you desire additional financing, please allow us the opportunity to be of service.

Cordially,

"SORRY! WE FORGOT TO CHARGE YOUR BANK CARD" LETTER

LETTER E-19

Used for inactive and large amounts over $100 to notify the customer of misposting.

Dear _____:

An audit of your account indicates we failed to charge you for a purchase made several months ago on your ABC Bank Credit Card. The purchase at _____ for $_____ made on _____ will appear on your next statement.

We sincerely regret any inconvenience caused by the delay in not adding this charge to your account at the proper time.

Cordially,

ABC Bank

CREDIT PAYMENT POSTING ERROR LETTER
LETTER E-20

Another problem in loan transactions.

Dear Mr. _____:

You were correct. We did receive your payment on the installment loan.

When we received your payment, we misread the account number. Actually, one of the digits was missing from the remittance slip. But that is our fault. The Bank policy requires a verification of the account number, and somehow we made an error.

We will do our best to prevent this from happening again. Sorry for any inconvenience and worry our error has caused.

Sincerely,

BANK ERROR—SENT PAST DUE NOTICE IN ERROR LETTER
LETTER E-21

A strong apology for a credit error is usually well received by the customer.

Dear _____:

You received a past due notice from us by mistake. Your account has always been current, as far as I am able to check the records. Because of the error in not applying your check to your account, we created this misunderatanding.

Please accept our apologies for the error and our thanks for sending a copy of your cancelled check. Our error was resolved once we received the information you sent.

Please be assured that your good credit record has been restored. We appreciate your calling this error to our attention.

Yours truly,

NOTICE OF BILLING ERROR RIGHTS LETTER

LETTER E-22

The following text which has been supplied by the Board of Governors of the Federal Reserve System, or one substantially similar, must be sent with each periodic statement required under Section 226.7(b)(1), if the creditor chooses to use the provisions of Section 226.7(d)(5) instead of mailing the text provided in Section 226.7(a)(9) semi-annually. This information was provided by the Board of Governors of the Federal Reserve System, Regulation Z amended to March 23, 1977.

IN CASE OF ERRORS OR INQUIRIES ABOUT YOUR BILL

Send your inquiry in writing (at creditor's option: on a separate sheet) so that the creditor receives it within 60 days after the bill was mailed to you. Your inquiry must include:

1. Your name and account number (if any);
2. A description of the error and why (to the extent you can explain) you believe it is an error; and
3. The dollar amount of the suspected error.

If you have authorized your creditor to automatically pay your bill from your checking or savings account, you can stop or reverse payment on any amount you think is wrong by mailing your notice so that the creditor receives it within 16 days after the bill was sent to you. You remain obligated to pay the parts of your bill not in dispute, but you do not have to pay any amount in dispute during the time the creditor is resolving the dispute. During that same time, the creditor may not take any action to collect disputed amounts or report disputed amounts as delinquent.

If you have a problem with property or services purchased with a credit card, you may have the right not to pay the remaining amount due on them if you first try in good faith to return them, or give the merchant a chance to correct the problem. There are two limitations on this right:

1. You must have bought them in your home state, or if not within your home state, within 100 miles of your current mailing address; and
2. The purchase price must have been more than $50.

However, these limitations do not apply if the merchant is owned or operated by the creditor, or if the creditor mailed you the advertisement for the property or services.

This is a summary of your rights; a full statement of your rights and the creditor's responsibilities under the Federal Fair Credit Billing Act will be sent to you both upon request and in response to a billing error notice.

BANK CREDIT CARD CUSTOMER INFORMATION LETTER

LETTER E-23

Bank credit card applications mailed to customers occasionally need additional information for processing. This is a form letter to expedite this process at lower cost.

Dear _____:

Thank you for requesting a _____ bank credit card. It will be a great shopping convenience.

However, additional information is required before we can complete your request. Please supply the information requested below and return this form in the enclosed envelope.

Sincerely,

If more space is needed, write on the back of this form. Please complete the items checked below.

( )   Your home address for the past four years.
         ( ) Present____Date____owned____rent____
         ( ) Former____Date____owned____rent____

( )   Your employer for the past four years. Full name and address.

         _____

( )   Bank references: checking, savings or loan)
         Bank_____Type Acct.____
         Bank_____Type Acct.____

EMPLOYMENT VERIFICATION LETTER

LETTER E-24

                     RE: (Applicant's Name)

Attention: Personnel Manager

In applying for a bank loan, the applicant has indicated present employment with your company. Your employee and the ABC

Bank would appreciate verification, and any comments useful in evaluating this loan application.

Your cooperation is greatly appreciated and will remain confidential. The applicant has granted his/her permission for release of this information.

Sincerely,

ABC Bank

You are permitted to release any and all information concerning my employment to the ABC Bank which might be useful in determining my credit status for a bank loan.

_____*(signed)*

_____

_____

(please do not detach)

Employed from_____ to_____ position_____
age____ dependents ____ salary _____ future job status
_____

_____   _____
(Authorized signature)   *(date)*

VERIFICATION OF CREDIT REFERENCES LETTER

LETTER E-25

Name
Address

Gentlemen:

In applying for a bank loan, the above person has given your name as a credit reference.

We will appreciate your advising us about the status of past credit record.

Your information will, of course, be held in strict confidence. Our loan customer has given you consent to provide this information.

Very truly yours,

Credit Dept.

To _____, please furnish the _____ Bank with the requested information concerning my credit dealings with your firm. Thank you.

Signed _____
(customer)

Date opened _____
High credit _____
Average balance _____
Present balance_____
Comments about payments _____

VERIFICATION OF SAVINGS LETTER

LETTER E-26

Date

Gentlemen:

You are authorized to give the _____ Bank information about my account at your bank. Your prompt handling of this request will be appreciated.

My account number is _____

Below is my signature as it appears on your records.

Signature _____
Name (*printed*) _____
Address _____
_____

_____FOR BANK USE ONLY_____

To _____ Bank
Account since _____
Average balance _____
Present balance _____
How maintained _____

By _____Title_____

VERIFICATION OF WRITTEN-OFF ACCOUNT LETTER

LETTER E-27

Used by a bank to verify accounts written-off and placed with a third party for collection. An excellent control technique that eliminates any discrepancies between the bank and the collection agency.

In connection with the examination of our accounting records, it would be appreciated if you would confirm for us the balance of your bank installment loan.

Our records indicate the accounts receivable from you is $_____ as of _____.

Your prompt attention to this request would be appreciated. A postage prepaid envelope is enclosed for your reply. This is not a request for payment, but a request to verify the amount outstanding.

DO NOT INCLUDE A PAYMENT WITH YOUR REPLY.

Thank you for your cooperation in this request.

Sincerely,

Internal Audit Unit

Confirmation:

The balance receivable from me of $_____ as of _____ is correct except as noted below:

_____
_____
_____

Date _____ Signed by _____
Acct. Number _____

CREDIT INQUIRY TO EMPLOYER LETTER

LETTER E-28

RE:

Gentlemen:

Your employee listed above has submitted an application for credit with the bank.

Will you, in confidence and without liability, confirm the statements appearing below? Our customer and your employee has authorized you to furnish us this information.

A self-addressed envelope is enclosed for your convenience.

Loan Dept.

My employer is authorized to furnish employment information to the _____ Bank for credit purposes.

Signed _____
Dept. No. _____ Badge No. _____

Position:
Salary:
Length of Service:
Signature of company official _____

REQUEST FOR FINANCIAL STATEMENT LETTER

LETTER E-29

Dear _____:

Our auditors require us to maintain in our files the financial statements of corporate borrowers.

Enclosed are two of our standard statement forms. Please complete them, retaining one copy for your files. It is important each line be completed. If no entry is to be entered on a line, use the word "None" for the amount.

If a public accountant has audited your records, we would appreciate receiving a copy.

Thank you for your prompt attention.

Very truly yours,

SECOND REQUEST FOR FINANCIAL STATEMENT LETTER

LETTER E-30

Dear _____:

Previously, we had sent you two copies of our standard financial statement forms to be completed and returned to the bank.

In the event that the original forms have been misplaced, I am enclosing two blank forms for your convenience. Please complete them according to the instructions.

With this information, the bank is better able to serve your banking needs. Your prompt return of the form is greatly appreciated.

Cordially,

"LITTLE THINGS MEAN A LOT" IN FINANCIAL STATEMENT ANALYSIS LETTER

LETTER E-31

A partial letter that examines the heart of the financial statement.

Dear _____:

Your gross profit percentage for the year was 2% higher than last year, which is an improvement for your business. However, since expenses increased 2.5% during the year, your net profit has declined.

The significance of these trends is more important than the actual figures. Your business may be in an increasingly tight cash position. This will prevent you from taking advantage of trade discounts which will increase your operating expenses. These trends sometimes go unnoticed to businessmen in day-to-day operation, so we are happy to analyze and direct your attention to those little things that can mean a lot in profits.

WORKING CAPITAL PARTIAL LETTER

LETTER E-32

A selected paragraph for the explanation of credit analysis of a finar cial statement.

Dear _____:

Every business requires adequate working capital. However, we feel that the consideration of establishing a line of credit so you can utilize short-term funds as required, would be advantageous to your business. It is difficult to build safe working capital that will parallel the growth of your business in the short-run. A short-term working capital line of credit will improve your financial position and will allow optimum use of immediate "opportunity" benefits.

FINANCIAL STATEMENT ANALYSIS PARTIAL LETTER

LETTER E-33

A partial letter to stress weakness in the financial statement.

Dear _____:

In order to continue your present line of credit, we want you to have a successful business future. In our examination of your comparative financial statements, we see a weakness that may prevent us from continuing your present line of credit.

We are looking at the present situation from your viewpoint as well as ours. We are willing to do whatever is necessary to assist you in getting your firm back on a sound financial basis. However, our loan review committee feels your situation is serious and deserves your immediate corrective attention.

ALTERNATE LOAN PLAN LETTER

LETTER E-34

A partial letter recommending a variation of an existing bank customer's loan plan.

Dear _____:

Inadequate capital is a most serious error for a new business, since success will require additional capital. You are building a successful, profitable business and we at ABC Bank are willing to consider stabilizing your financial statements.

It appears from our review, that you will need at least $27,000 in additional working capital. If we provide a loan, it should be a long-term five year loan, because it can be easily repaid from net profits after taxes. If the repayments were to exceed net earnings, it would impair the working capital. Longer than five years is not advisable, but if you have that extraordinary year as anticipated, early retirement of the working capital loan would be in your best interests.

REMEDIAL ANALYSIS OF STATEMENT LETTER

LETTER E-35

The partial letter that solved a business problem and saved a business from an anticipated bankruptcy.

Dear _____:

The solution to your business problem is not additional loans. Why should you pay the cost of borrowing, in order to carry the excessive past due situation revealed by the analysis of your financial statement? If you are afraid to stress payment terms for fear of losing an account, then you are better off without that account; especially after it is 90 and 100 days past due. These accounts will only destroy your business. If these firms are worthwhile, they can pay your invoices or borrow money to do so. If they are unable to do either, you made a mistake to extend credit to them initially.

Since the ABC Bank has a major stake in your future, we will be happy to supply the services of one of our credit specialists to assist in revising your credit policies, and to offer direction in liquidating the serious accounts receivable problem.

REASON FOR FINANCIAL STATEMENT LETTER

LETTER E-36

A partial letter that defines the major elements of the financial statement.

Dear _____:

Your bank payment record is a major basis of extending business credit. However, we consider another vital factor to be the condition of your financial statement, which is the basis of the continuing banking service we offer you. After comparison of your year-to-year statement, we attempt to determine the future trend and advise you accordingly. The basic comparisons are the relationship between your current assets and current liabilities, and the relationship between your total liabilities and net worth.

As your banker, we are in a unique position of having access to financial data from many similar businesses. It becomes easy for us to spot adverse trends that can be corrected before the situation affects loan repayments and business profits.

DENIAL OF INCREASED LINE OF CREDIT LETTER

LETTER E-37

A partial letter that defines the refusal to increase the present line of credit.

Dear _____:

Your request to increase the present line of credit is simply borrowing against your future ability to pay, which will be a continuation of a weak financial expansion plan. Perhaps you need to defer the contemplated expansion until next fall, in order to consolidate your present successful operation. Our bank loan committee does not feel they can safely recommend the increase. When we receive your next year-end financial statement, we will review it. If you still feel strongly about your proposal at that time, enclose with the statement a copy of your budget and expansion forecast.

GROUP *F* LETTERS

Thirty-seven Letters and Partial Letters that Answer the Most Difficult Bank Collection Problems

The collection letters presented in this group represent the work-horses of the credit operation in the bank. These letters are conceived to get the money into the bank and to reduce the delinquency problem while maintaining customer goodwill. The balance between getting paid and maintaining goodwill requires new collection approaches. But banks that do achieve these two goals report improved collection results.

According to studies of bankruptcy trends and characteristics, one cause of increased losses in this area results from the uncaring attitude upon the part of the collection personnel. The letters compiled in this group, provide an array of alternate collection responses that have been "field-tested" in banking situations. A stronger stress on empathy—the new collection technique—is displayed in early collection stage letters.

The difficult collection situations require a continuity of message coupled with increased pressure for success. The many choices of letters allow for variety, which enables the collection specialist to select tailor-made situation, problem-solving letters. From this group, the bank can establish a complete new series of collection messages that can reduce delinquency.

"WE'LL ACCEPT A LOWER PAYMENT" COLLECTION LETTER

LETTER F-1

A unique letter rejecting the customer's proposed offer to make lower payments, but giving a workable alternative.

> Dear _____:
>
> Your letter explaining your temporary loss of income helps us to understand your personal situation. We want to be of assistance in your financial recovery. Of course, you understand that it is important to give this obligation priority.
>
> Please send the payment of $___ as you mentioned in your letter, at once, to demonstrate your good intentions. However, this payment plan as you proposed is unacceptable to the bank. We feel it would not be in the best interest of you or us.
>
> The bank loan committee has reviewed your letter, and has recommended the following repayment schedule until your income situation improves; thereby enabling you to correct any remaining past due indebtedness.
>
> 1. Your acknowledged payment $———— at once.
> 2. Weekly/Monthly payments of $_____ starting (*date*).
>
> This special payment plan should aid you through a difficult period of time. We will be expecting the first payment in a few days.
>
> Cordially,
>
> ABC Bank

PAYMENT EQUALS PEACE OF MIND LETTER

LETTER F-2

Collection letters with appeal to emotional benefits have strong pulling power. The bank using this collection reminder found a 14 percent increase in collections returned with this letter over the letter that was previously used at two month delinquency.

Account No.
Amount Due.

Dear _____:

It is in the spirit of fair play that we remind you, once again, of the past due nature of your loan.

The ABC Bank *enjoys* having you as a customer. We hope you enjoy borrowing from us. However, we must ask that you send the amount due.

Not only will we be happy to receive your payment . . . but we'll bet that you will be relieved to get the loan current and off your mind.

Send the payment today or pay at any branch of the bank.

Cordially,

ABC Bank

LUXURY OF CREDIT COLLECTION LETTER

LETTER F-3

An innovative bank credit card collection letter.

Dear _____:

We don't think you really want to give up the luxury of your bank credit card after using it since 19___.

As holidays and birthdays approach, it is convenient and useful for special and emergency purchases. As your bank, we want you to enjoy the luxury of the credit card. However, the current payment is past due. This will require us to ask for the return of the credit card if the payment is not sent within the next five days.

Keep your bank credit card and send us the small payment now due.

Sincerely,

ABC Bank

"SAVE YOUR PROPERTY" COLLECTION LETTER

LETTER F-4

A unique letter that builds concern and motivates the borrower to pay the account.

Dear _____:

You indicated when we approved your installment loan that you made a wise purchase. Your property is still an important possession.

We must insist upon the past due payments being sent at once. If we do not receive the required payments, the total loan balance shall be due and payable according to your loan agreement. If we do not receive the scheduled payments or the total balance by the first of next month, we will have no other choice except to repossess the property in accordance with the security agreement.

Make your payment at any branch of the bank and protect your interest in the mortgaged property.

Cordially,

ABC Bank

COLLECT WITH EMPATHY LETTER

LETTER F-5

An unusual collection letter to a bank customer that has sold products to the bank in the past—the injection of empathy collected the past due installments at once.

Dear _____:

When we purchased your products for use here at the bank, you expected prompt payment of the invoice. I checked the file to find that the bank paid your invoice "As agreed." You were justified in expecting our payment promptly. Won't you treat your bank loan in the same manner that we treated your invoice? The bank and your business have the same cash flow requirements. Only by payments from our trusted and valued customers can we fulfill our continuing obligations to the community.

On the basis of mutual respect, don't you think that you should reciprocate by clearing up the past due installments?

I greatly appreciate your consideration.

Cordially,

ABC Bank

"WHEN THE TELEPHONE CALLS DON'T GET THROUGH" LETTER

LETTER F-6

A special letter to the delinquent customer who avoids your telephone calls. This letter eliminated the "Out of the office" problem.

Dear _____:

I tried to call you several times about the serious condition of your bank loan. Perhaps I am more concerned than you are about the delinquency that is mounting rapidly.

Your office regularly informs me that you are "Busy and not available" for my calls. Certainly, I am pleased that your business is growing successfully. The overdue payments are possibly caused by your oversight and your new problems of operating a successful business.

However, I need not tell you the value of good bank relations for a growing business. Therefore, you can appreciate my concern for the tardiness of the most recent payments on your bank loan.

If you can't get your payments sent within five days, be certain to contact me at once.

Very truly yours,

ABC Bank

"KEEP YOUR BUYING POWER"—COLLECTION LETTER

LETTER F-7

An innovative bank credit card collection letter that stresses the benefit of perpetual use (if kept current) of a credit line.

Dear _____:

Did you know . . .
your bank credit card is a most valuable possession?

Not everyone is entitled to a bank credit card. Only after careful review of your request did we issue your credit card with a credit limit of $500.

Did you know that a mere payment of $25 per month will give you credit buying power in excess of $2,400 over the next ten years?

Don't lose your special buying power! Bring your account current, *now*.

Cordially,

ABC Bank

PROMISED PAYMENT DATE REMINDER LETTER

LETTER F-8

The use of this payment date reminder was sent five days prior to the promised payment date. The results showed a 32 percent increase in payments made on the promised date.

IMPORTANT DATE _____

You promised to pay us on the above date.
Your promised payment will be expected.

ABC Bank

PAYMENT DUE REMINDER LETTER

LETTER F-9

Another excellent payment date reminder *mailed* seven days prior to the billing or installment due date for delinquent accounts.

Account No.
Due date
Amount due

Dear _____:

We want to remind you that a payment on your loan with *ABC Bank* is due on the date indicated above.
Please mail your payment on or before the due date. Payment may also be made at any branch of the bank.

Very sincerely yours,

BROKEN PROMISE PAYMENT LETTER

LETTER F-10

After institution of this broken promise payment letter, the response with payments increased upwards of 17 percent. The letter is sent five days after the payment is due.

Dear ⸻:

You broke your promise!

I believed you when you agreed to send the payment of $⸻ on ⸻. I even sent you a reminder prior to the due date for this payment.

Five days ago you were to send the payment. Still, no payment after today's mail. At the first opportunity, I will review your broken promise with my bank supervisor.

Please call me at once to inform me if payment has already been sent.

Very truly yours,

PARTIAL PAYMENT LETTER

LETTER F-11

A letter stressing urgency that breaks the partial pay habit.

                                        Amount due
Dear Customer:

Your recent payment has been applied to your loan.

However, this payment is only a partial payment of the past due amount. We must insist that you send the remaining amount due at once.

If you are unable to send this amount at once, we urge you to call the bank Loan Department within the next five days to make definite arrangements for the payment of the amount due.

Your partial payment is a start in restoring your account to a good credit payment record.

Installment Loan Dept.

SKIPPED PAYMENT COLLECTION LETTER

LETTER F-12

A collection letter for the customer that is paying you, then skips a payment and then pays again.

Dear ⸻:

You have just skipped a payment again.

After reviewing your pay history for the past six months, I realize you are attempting to solve a difficult financial situation. However, skipping a payment and catching up later only to repeat the problem, ruins your good pay history.

Wouldn't it be better to make each scheduled payment as due? Your obligation to the bank is a major financial commitment to which you must give priority consideration. Stop in to see me if I can be of assistance.

Your next payment of $____ is due at the bank no later than _____. We expect your payment on or before that date.

Cordially,

ABC Bank

SLOW PAY HABIT-BREAKER LETTER

LETTER F-13

The following letter offers the reader a substantial benefit for prompt payment. This letter brings results.

Dear _____:

Thank you for your recent payment.

However, you are still one payment in arrears according to your installment loan schedule.

If you establish a habit of being slow in remitting payments, you will harm your credit rating with us. When you ask the bank for your next car loan, we will consider your payment habits on the current loan.

A self-addressed envelope is enclosed for your convenience in sending the past due payment at this time.

Very truly yours,

PARTIAL PAYMENT AGREEMENT LETTER

LETTER F-14

A form letter to acknowledge a partial payment agreement that reinforces the payment promise.

Dear _____:

We have accepted your agreement to make temporary partial payments.

Your present balance is $＿＿. Starting ＿＿＿＿ 19＿＿,
you agreed to send $＿＿ each week/month.

This special plan was made for your convenience, and includes
an amount that will bring your account to a current status in
＿＿＿＿＿ months. Then you will be able to resume your normal loan payment of $＿＿.

Protect your agreement—make the scheduled payments on
time!

ABC Bank

PARTIAL PAYMENT RESPONSE LETTER

LETTER F-15

This form letter can be computerized for inexpensive mid-period
dunning, in order to bring in additional payments before the actual
billing date. Upon receipt of a partial payment, the computer is automatically programmed to print this notice acknowledging the payment and advising that additional payment is due.

Thank you . . .
For your *partial* payment.

However, it was not sufficient to bring your loan current. For
your convenience, we have shown the payment due this
month. Please send it by return mail or pay at any branch of the
ABC Bank.

Account No.
Balance
Amount Due
Date

REAL ESTATE MORTGAGE COLLECTION LETTER

LETTER F-16

Showing concern for the customer will bring results.

Dear Customer:

Wouldn't it be easier . . .

To make the overdue payment on your mortgage loan now . . .
instead of later, when you will be required to make two payments on your loan?

Once a real estate loan falls a month behind, we are worried . . . as you must be. Soon you will be required to make two payments.

So for your own best interest, mail your payment at once—including the late charge. If this is impossible, telephone us to explain your situation. You will find us understanding and perhaps able to offer a solution.

Bring your mortgage payment current—now!

Cordially,

ABC Bank

NOTICE OF INTENT TO FORECLOSE REAL ESTATE LETTER

LETTER F-17

Dear _____:

Your real estate loan is now past due _____ payments.

The total amount due is $____. If payment to reinstate your loan account is not received in the above amount prior to _____, then an additional payment of $____ must be added to the amount due.

If you fail to respond to this notice, it will be necessary to initiate foreclosure.

We may be able to help if you contact us immediately, and arrange an immediate appointment to discuss possible remedies for the delinquency.

The adverse effects of foreclosure include added costs, and the loss of your house.

Your house is probably your most valuable investment—protect it. It is up to you to make a decision. Time is vital!

Very truly yours,

"ONLY HOURS TO PAY"—COLLECTION LETTER

LETTER F-18

A unique notice creating urgency for serious delinquency.

> Certified Mail No.
> Balance Due

Dear _____:

Regarding your installment loan with the bank:

—48 HOUR NOTICE—

You have failed to respond to previous requests for payment of this loan. We must therefore advise you that unless *PAYMENT IN FULL* is received at any branch of the bank within 48 hours from receipt of this letter—we will refer your loan account to our staff attorney for any action he recommends.

Either contact your attorney and advise him of our decision, or make *PAYMENT AT ONCE*.

ABC Bank

DEMAND FOR PAYMENT IN FULL LETTER

LETTER F-19

Re: Total Balance $_____.

Dear _____:

Unless we receive payment of the total balance in full within five days, we shall assume you did not intend to settle this loan in a friendly manner. In five days we will proceed accordingly.

Send your payment NOW.

ABC Bank

FIVE-DAY COLLECTION DEMAND LETTER

LETTER F-20

This collection letter develops urgency in customer response.

Dear _____:

You have chosen to ignore our many requests for payment on your installment loan with the bank. This is our final demand.

We would have been happy to have arranged a monthly schedule of payments, but you have refused to cooperate in any payment plan.

Therefore, your entire balance is due in full. We must have payment in full within the next five days. The balance due is _____.

We dislike losing a customer in this way, but it has been caused by your negligence. Remember, *FIVE DAYS*.

Very truly yours,

"WE'LL TELL" COLLECTION LETTER

LETTER F-21

Remind the borrower that the co-indorser or co-signer of the bank loan can be brought into the picture if delinquency continues.

Dear _____:

Your bank loan was signed by a co-indorser. As of this date, we have not informed the co-indorser of the potential liability because of your default.

We would prefer that you bring the past due payments up to date by sending within five days the amount of $____. After _____, we will be obligated to contact the co-indorser to insure that the balance is paid in full. Will you give this matter your immediate attention? Please send the payments due at once.

Sincerely,

ABC Bank

CO-MAKER NOTIFICATION LETTER

LETTER F-22

Collection follow-up to the co-maker, co-indorser or co-signer for a bank loan. Follow-up to letter F-21 is the key to collection. Co-makers become effective collection people.

Date

Dear _____:

We regret to inform you that . . .

The loan to _____ is now in default. You are being advised as the co-indorser for the bank loan.

We did advise _____ that we are obligated to contact you if payment is not made by today's date. Since we have received no response or payment from _____, we must advise you of the default in payments.

Please call our office for an appointment, so you may personally make arrangements to pay the balance in full. If any payments are received by us, we will advise you.

Sincerely,

OVERDRAFT ACCOUNT LETTER

LETTER F-23

A firing-line collection letter. First in a series for overdraft banking.

Dear Customer:

We are pleased that you are taking advantage of your overdraft credit line. However, our recent bank statement mailed to you reflects that you have not made the required payments equal to 1/24th of your credit line, during the month since your last statement.

We assume that this may have been an oversight on your part and that the required payments will be made shortly to correct the delinquency. If there is any reason for delay in adjusting this situation, please let me know the circumstances as soon as possible.

If you have already made the required payment, please disregard this letter.

Cordially,

OVERDRAFT COLLECTION LETTER

LETTER F-24

The second reminder to good customers to be used as a preprinted form letter.

Dear _____:

We hope that you are finding the overdraft credit line a convenient service of the bank.

However, our recent reminder apparently has not been responsive. Soon you will be required to make two payments in order to bring your credit line account current.

Obviously, this is merely an oversight on your part. Please make the required payment so that you may continue to enjoy this unique service.

If the required payment has been made, accept our thanks for a prompt response.

Sincerely,

SKIP TRACE INQUIRY LETTER

LETTER F-25

An inquiry to references on the credit application.

> We are receiving return mail from a customer of the bank.
>
> You were given as a personal/credit reference by:
>
>> *Name*
>> *Address*
>
> At the time of the application, our customer's address was:
>
>> *Address*
>
> We would appreciate any information that can be given by you to aid in our locating them; so we may contact them and forward our mail.
>
> If you are still in contact with them, please complete the form below:
>
>> *Present home address*
>
> Thank you for your assistance. Enclosed is a self-addressed envelope for your reply.
>
> Very truly yours,
>
> ABC Bank

THE "LOST CUSTOMER" FOUND LETTER

LETTER F-26

After return mail—a little skip tracing—give the "found" customer a graceful face-saving out.

> Account No.
> Amount due
>
> Dear Customer:
>
> We sincerely regret the circumstances that caused your recent bank notices to be delayed in reaching you at your current address.
>
> To bring your account up to date, you need to make the payment stated above.

If you have any questions concerning your loan, please contact me.

Very truly yours,

Installment Loan Dept.
ABC Bank

COMPUTER DUN SERIES

The following computerized letters demonstrate continuity and increased collection pressure.

50-DAY LETTER

LETTER F-27

CAUTION . . . Don't jeopardize your credit standing. We feel that our bank plan is liberal and convenient for you. However, when you fail to make payments, you defeat the purpose of this plan. Your payments accumulate and a larger amount becomes due.

Please send the amount below NOW to bring your account current. If payment has already been mailed, thank you.

Account No.
Balance
Amount Due
Date

70-DAY LETTER

LETTER F-28

URGENT . . . You have ignored our earlier request for payment. If you have not already sent payment, it is imperative that you immediately pay the AMOUNT DUE to bring your account current. Preserve your good credit standing with your bank by sending the payment at once.

Account No.
Balance
Amount Due
Date

80-DAY COLLECTION LETTER

LETTER F-29

NOTICE . . . Before our collector attempts to call you, we want to take this opportunity to request payment on an impersonal basis.

Your account is serious to us. We are concerned that you have not paid previously. Therefore, send the payment as requested below.

Account No.
Balance
Amount Due
Date

100-DAY COLLECTION LETTER

LETTER F-30

STOP . . .

It is important that we gain your agreement in maintaining your credit account according to the credit terms.

We do not want to continue collection activity. But without your immediate payment of the AMOUNT DUE, we will be forced to proceed with further collection procedures.

Account No.
Balance
Amount Due
Date

110-DAY COLLECTION LETTER

LETTER F-31

FINAL OPPORTUNITY . . .

Liquidate your obligation before we are compelled to refer your account to our Legal Department.

Unless we receive your payment within the next ten days, we *shall* refer your record to our Legal Department with instructions to protect the interest of the bank.

You should protect your interest by sending the payment. DO
IT NOW!

Account No.
Balance
Amount Due
Date

SIX PARTIAL LETTERS—SELECTED PARAGRAPHS
LETTERS F-32 to F-37

Unique situations and the desire to inject individuality into your
collection letters are the functions of these selected paragraphs that
have been tested in past collection messages.

LETTER F-32

The length of time your account has gone unpaid is of great
concern to us. The amount is small, but I am sure you are
aware that many small, unpaid balances can result in large
losses for the bank.

LETTER F-33

As one with an established credit reputation, you will do yourself a favor by paying the small loan balance still past due.
Protect your credit reputation with prompt remittance.

LETTER F-34

Your broken promises display a total lack of concern for your
loan. You have convinced us that any extra effort on our part
will be a waste of valuable time.

LETTER F-35

Perhaps your delinquent loan can be refinanced through
another institution. We would appreciate your efforts to release
us of the obligation of continuing as your lending banker.

LETTER F-36

Since you are no longer residing in our service area, we will be
forced to engage the services of a collection agency in
_____ that will be in personal contact with you. Avoid this
action by sending your payment for the balance in full.

LETTER F-37

We wish to be fair and give you an opportunity to settle the past due amount on your installment loan. Your immediate payment is required.

GROUP *G* LETTERS

Twenty-five Difficult Personal Situation Bank Letters

The reputation and status of bankers invites others in the community to ask for involvement by bankers in a great many non-business situations. Because the bank can be linked to the request, the response to difficult personal situations requires careful analysis and planning to properly communicate an effective answer. Saying "no" to important people to the bank and to those who can mold a banker's career, must be said with positive attitude letters.

The personal situation letter is not an easy letter to write. As you review the selected messages in this group, you will find excellent letters that tell officials, for example, that they are wrong, but offer an important face-saving conveyance that can influence a gentle change of opinion. After all, in most personal situations there are generally two viewpoints. Neither viewpoint may be totally incorrect. An awareness of another's viewpoint will make the difficult personal situation letter more understandable and more effective.

The following letters will provide the properly balanced response to all the major encounters by bankers. Prompt replies to the personal situations are important for maintaining good relations with those people who count on you for special support.

SAYING "NO" TO CITY COMMISSIONER LETTER

LETTER G-1

Anyone can dash off a "Yes" reply. But the art of saying "No" is just that—an art. The great leaders down through history mastered this art. Successful bankers must have a flair for the art of saying "No." After all, banking is saying "No" at the right time to the right people.

Dear _____:

Your ideas on how the bank may better serve the community are sound, and worth consideration. Your letter was reviewed by our management staff to determine how we, as the city's leading bank, might put your ideas into practice.

Knowing how busy you are as a forward-thinking member of the City Commission and member of the Zoning Board, we do know that your ideas are not lightly suggested to the business community. However, you do realize that your concrete suggestions concerning the innovative, city-wide loan program described in your letter will require a major policy decision for this bank. Some members of our bank loan committee are more conservative-thinking than you. Therefore, a committee was established to consider how to implement some parts of your suggested program.

It is unfortunate that the bank does not have the expertise to implement your program at this time. Since the margin is narrow between what the bank pays for the use of funds and the current lending rate, we must be conservative. One of our concerns is keeping your valued trust as a stockholder and bank depositor. This concern is balanced by our requirement to serve the community with innovative programs such as you suggested.

As the bank becomes involved in more lending activity, we will be needing your help and ideas. Certainly, you will be doing the bank and the city a great service by suggesting innovative, city-wide programs. Thank you for giving us an opportunity to review your suggestions.

Sincerely,

ABC Bank
President

SAYING "NO" TO POLITICAL CONTRIBUTIONS LETTER

LETTER G-2

A difficult situation arises when a friend or close associate requests political contributions.

Dear _____:

Thank you for your letter/telephone call of February 10, 19___.
I am delighted to see that you are running for city council. Also,
I hear you have the support of a fine group of men and women
working for you.

Because of my banking function, it is difficult to financially support any candidate directly. In order to maintain a nonpartisan
position, I have always made it a policy to contribute directly to
the political parties and not to contribute directly to any candidate. My policy is certainly difficult to maintain when such a fine
candidate as you is working hard for the community.

I wish you the very best of success in your campaign. There is
no doubt in my mind that you will make a fine city councilman.

Kindest regards,

PERSUADING THE DISMISSAL OF SUIT LETTER

LETTER G-3

The following letter averted a quarter million dollar countersuit and
saved the writer over a thousand dollars in disputed charges.

Dear _____:

I am writing to you confidentially as a former DEF Company
customer.

Our dispute has been set for trial Wednesday, April 14, 19___.
Why your company has chosen this course of action is a shock
to good judgment, since the amount due is in dispute. The
documents submitted with the court papers by your company
support the error.

It appears that the DEF Company engages in unorthodox tac-
tics to enforce payment regardless of whether the amount is
properly owed. The mental anguish and suffering over this matter must be compounded many-fold throughout the country by
other individuals who are caught in the web of billing errors.

I've been informed that the DEF Company has violated state
and federal rules and laws in collection activity against us. Ap-

parently that matters not to your organization. However, adverse activity cannot be changed at DEF Company unless you request an ethical operation. It would be the better part of valor to dismiss the suit against us as we have requested in the petition. We can resolve our problems privately, outside the public eye of courtroom trials. To be sure, we will be in attendance to present our case on April 14, 19____.

I hope you will review the records and save the DEF Company the expense of spending a day in court.

Cordially,

REFUSAL TO DONATE TO CHARITY LETTER

LETTER G-4

Saying "No" to charity donations without offending your friends.

Dear _____:

Thank you for your kind letter. It was so nice to hear from you again.

Because of the strict standards established by the Board of Directors, the ABC Bank is not permitted to make additional donations to charitable causes this year. Each year, the Board reviews our community obligations and determines the amount of contribution for each approved charity.

I'm sorry that the bank is not in a position to add any new charities to our family of community services. I know your charity is worthwhile, and wish you the best in going over your fund drive goal.

Sincerely,

REQUEST TO CAR DEALER FOR PROPER SERVICE TO CONSUMER BANK CUSTOMER LETTER

LETTER G-5

When the bank is caught in the middle between the borrower and the merchant, the bank walks a tightrope between two bank customers.

Dear _____:

It is a pleasure to handle the financing of your agency's new and used autos. We look forward to a long business relationship.

You are probably aware of the consumer challenges to the "holder in due course" concept; under which we agree to finance your customer purchases without recourse to you, the dealer. Recently, we received a complaint from a valued bank customer of twelve years, who felt she was proper in withholding future installment loan payments on an auto recently purchased from your agency. The purchase of any product is independent of the financing, as we rely on the integrity of the auto dealers to handle the servicing and warranty problems when they arise. We are not able, nor do we want to, enter into the marketplace between you and your customers. Banking is our specialty, and auto sales and service—at which you have an excellent reputation—is yours.

Please review the service complaint of our mutual customer, Ms. _____, residing at _____. I am sure that a complete explanation of the problems will be beneficial. Since the auto is under warranty, perhaps a complete inspection will resolve the unpleasant driving difficulties that the customer is experiencing.

We do not desire to "stand" in the middle between you and your customer relationship. Your understanding of our unique position is greatly appreciated.

Sincerely,

HELPING THE CONSUMER BANK CUSTOMER WITH DEFECTIVE PURCHASE LETTER

LETTER G-6

When the customer threatens to withhold payments because of defects in the purchase financed by the bank, a special resolution is needed by the bank.

Dear _____:

Service to our banking customers is most important to us. We greatly appreciate your letter informing us of problems with the recent auto purchase that was financed with the bank.

We want you to enjoy any item purchased on our installment loan plan. Of course, you realize that we do not control the auto dealer, and can only add our weight to yours in requesting a fair settlement of your service problems. The purchase of the auto and the financing of the auto are separate and independent transactions. We agreed to arrange your financing, because you are a valued customer of the bank. At no time do we investigate or inquire about the soundness of your purchase. You are always free to select any merchant you choose for purchases. We, of course, stand ready to arrange financing just for you, because of your excellent twelve year record with the bank.

Rest assured that we did call the dealer on your behalf, in order to arrange an appointment for you to discuss the auto defects with Mr. _____, the Service Manager. We are delighted to have an opportunity to do this for you. You should be able to resolve the service problems quickly, since your auto is still under warranty. Mr. _____ wants you to call him personally at _____, so he can review the service situation.

Thank you for another opportunity to be of service.

Cordially,

REPLY TO THE UNJUSTIFIED POLICY COMPLAINT LETTER

LETTER G-7

Policy complaints written to bank officers must be answered with a courteous reply. Banking goodwill may pay off in the uncertain future.

Dear Mr. Delmar Jones:

You are correct that the name D. Jones sounds impersonal and abbreviated. But in preparing welcome letters to our new customers, we are restricted in the number of spaces allowed for the names by the computerized name and address label.

Of course, if we changed the D. to Delmar because we preferred it, we would offend others who prefer to have business mail addressed with the initial only. A friend of mine has the reverse problem of yours, so I understand the comments in your letter. My friend's first name is Conley which is a fine name, but he prefers "Sam." He becomes upset whenever a mailing is sent using his full name. His preference is for receiving mail using only the initial.

We believe banking means more than loans-deposits-withdrawals. That is why we wanted to welcome you as a new customer. Also, we think of our customers as friends. Only among friends do we feel concern for the many slights in life. We hope you will forgive us for our unintended slight. Please stop by the bank on your next trip; we want you to get to like us.

Cordially,

SAYING "NO"—BANK CANNOT SUPPLY
REQUESTED ITEM LETTER

LETTER G-8

When an inquiry is received for several units of a gift premium that cannot be sold, this letter is appropriate.

Dear _____ :

Thank you for your interesting letter.

The ABC Bank does not sell any of the items listed in our advertising brochure. The items you requested are extremely useful and that is why we offer them as gifts.

Some hardware or department stores should be able to supply the items desired. You might try the mail order department of one of your local stores. Perhaps it is a stocked item or a special order that can be accepted by the store.

You should have little difficulty finding the items you want for your family. We appreciate your letter indicating your interest in our gift premium.

Cordially,

BANKER UNABLE TO COMPLY—CHANGED BANK
EMPLOYMENT LETTER

LETTER G-9

When a request for assistance or information to a banker is forwarded, an appropriate response is necessary.

Dear _____ :

Thank you for your letter which was forwarded to me by my previous employee.

In _____ 19____, I resigned my position at the ZXY Bank to accept my current position with the ABC Bank. Consequently, I cannot assist you with the requested information.

Your letter and a copy of my response is being sent to my very able replacement at the ZXY Bank, Mr. _____ , Assistant Vice-President. I have no doubt that Mr. _____ can adequately service your request.

Your letter and kind words are appreciated. If I can be of further assistance, please do not hesitate to contact me.

Sincerely,

CRITICAL OF STOCK ANALYST'S
STOCK RECOMMENDATION LETTER

LETTER G-10

Responding to a stock analyst with further information to support a critical aspect of the stocks under consideration.

Dear _____:

First, I want to thank you for the statistical material on the performance of the five stocks under consideration.

Your analysis of recent developments and further prospects is useful in our investment planning. However, your analysis of the _____ Corporation was surprising. The capitalization reflects a debt capitalization of 63.4%, as compared to stock and surplus capitalization of 36.6%.

This company is presently selling at $20, on a downward range of $25 to $18 during the past twelve years. The price earnings ratio at 10.5% and the current yield at 5.9% are attractive inducements for consideration. But the excessive debt capitalization can cause future earnings problems if the economy weakens. We question your comment, "the company has a relatively strong capital position."

Please give this particular stock further research. The relatively high debt capitalization could be a danger signal. We hesitate to make further purchases, and perhaps should lighten our portfolios of this particular stock.

Your comments and further research are appreciated by the ABC Bank.

Cordially,

CRITICAL RESPONSE TO STOCK ANALYST'S
REPORT ON BANK LETTER

LETTER G-11

When a stock service reports an unfavorable remark about the bank.

Dear _____:

Your investment service reports are avidly read by us at the ABC Bank. The analysis presented by you is highly reliable and respected by many in the investment area. Your analysis and comments can have a major effect on price fluctuations.

The price of the ABC Bank stock dropped several points immediately following release of your recent analysis of our banking progress. We feel the offhand comment, "ABC Bank is located in a geographical area which offers little potential for future growth," is a statement that we cannot allow to stand. Since the statement is detrimental to our banking plans and image, we want to appraise you of factors that do not limit our banking, geographically.

The opening of our London office recently will aid our international business. We offer complete domestic and international banking services. Also, the ABC Bank acts as a factor, and purchases accounts receivable. We have been successful in aggressively seeking deposits during the past three years.

Perhaps in a future issue of your investment service report you will correct the misstatement. We would like to provide you with detailed and highly interesting recent developments at the ABC Bank, which should provide valuable insight into current banking.

We appreciate your interest in reporting the performance of our banking services.

Cordially,

COMPLIMENTARY ON STOCK ANALYST'S REPORT OF BANK LETTER

LETTER G-12

When a great report on the bank is issued, it pays to mention your favorable reaction.

Dear _____:

Your recent report with favorable comments about our banking services is sincerely appreciated. We have just completed a future development plan which is enclosed for your information.

As you will note from the development plan, we are rapidly expanding our branch system for greater banking service. The rapid growth in loans, and high yields available on securities and loans, is expected to continue. The increase in the prime rate boosted the gain in earnings last year, and we expect earnings to increase less dramatically this year, due to the reduced prime rate in effect during most of the year. The bank will benefit from the long-range strong loan demand with a healthy increase in net operating earnings.

It is always a pleasure to read favorable reports about our bank. We hope the enclosed information is of value to your reporting service, and look forward to your personal comments about the ABC Bank.

Cordially,

SAYING "NO"—BUDGETARY MATTER PREVENT LOAN LETTER

LETTER G-13

Discussing a budgeted potential investment is a difficult area to enter without adequate explanation.

Dear _____:

The success of your company brings new opportunities for expansion. The ABC Bank is pleased to be in a position to lend you its funds and experience gained from similar situations with other banking customers.

Your alternative situation to lease the _____ department or continue to operate the department directly, is properly presented by your budget analysis reflecting a net financial advantage of $8,000 annually; over the opportunity to lease the department as a concession.

However, the new product line you propose can be substituted for the present line even more profitably, without the need to build onto the present facility. From your data, we are able to deduce the following:

Contribution of new product line	$56,000
Loss of present product line	42,000
Net advantage of new products	$14,000

The loan funds to merchandise both product lines will not bring you a rate of return that can be considered favorable to your operation.

We would recommend that the new product line be instituted in place of the existing line. You will not need the increased debt which could weaken your financial position as you attempt to service both product lines. Because of the more favorable profitability, the new merchandise should be selected in place of the new line now being handled by this department. We hope this is a beneficial analysis for you.

Cordially,

SAYING "NO" WITH A BETTER SUGGESTION TO THE REAL ESTATE PROBLEM LETTER

LETTER G-14

A letter stating the specific reason for saying "No" when income is not sufficient for a requested real estate purchase.

Dear _____:

Thank you for considering ABC Bank for your financing.

In real estate mortgage lending, nationwide studies support the fact that a certain relationship does exist between an individual's income, fixed monthly expense, and loan amount. Our maximum real estate mortgage is based on two and one-half times the annual income. Our experience shows that a mortgage payment should not exceed 20% of the total monthly income. Since your income combined with your spouse's income, at present, does not meet either of these requirements for the requested loan; you can understand our reluctance to impose an additional financial burden on your family. The amount of the monthly mortgage payments will not serve your best interests.

Perhaps your real estate agent can assist you in locating a residence suitable to your needs that will require a smaller loan. We will be pleased to assist in arranging a mortgage that will be more favorable to your earning power, and also help you achieve your desired goal of home ownership.

Cordially,

OFFER OF BANK PARTICIPATION WITH THE SMALL BUSINESS ADMINISTRATION LETTER

LETTER G-15

When a business solution suggests SBA joining with the bank, or a guarantee for part of a bank loan.

Dear _____:

Your business proposal to purchase the wholesale business is well-planned. As the manager of the existing business, you certainly are an experienced technician.

You will find the ownership of a business completely different from being the manager. With the limited amount of capital you have presently, you will not be able to complete the purchase with our commercial loan formula. However, under the Small Business Agency loan guarantee, we would be willing to lend you the higher amount that your business proposal requires.

If the SBA guarantee is a suitable alternative, please call me so we can contact the agency for the necessary processing forms. We may be able to solve your banking needs.

Cordially,

EMERGENCY BANK TRANSFER OF FUNDS LETTER

LETTER G-16

Solving emergencies by banking services can lighten the stress with a pleasant personal touch.

Dear ——————:

Your request was handled immediately.

Funds from your account were transferred to our correspondent bank in San Francisco today by wire. Your son can pick up the funds at —————— Bank upon his arrival Monday in San Francisco.

We are happy to be able to aid in eliminating the financial crisis experienced by your son on his vacation trip. Be sure and tell John to have lunch at the little restaurant across the street from the —————— Bank. It has always been one of my favorite spots in San Francisco. I am sure it will help make his vacation more pleasant.

Best wishes to you and your son.

Cordially,

RELEASE OF ASSIGNMENT LETTER

LETTER G-17

A regular letter that must be part of the bank's communication portfolio.

Dear ——————:

The ABC Bank hereby releases any assignment on policy number 2233445561 of the XYZ Life Insurance Company issued to John Doe. The ABC Bank holds harmless the XYZ Life Insurance Company for termination of this assignment to the ABC Bank.

Sincerely,

MATURITY OF FARMER'S LOAN LETTER

LETTER G-18

Special banking considerations are encountered in processing farm loans.

Dear _____:

With spring just around the corner, you will be involved in extensive farming activities.

Also, it is the time to review your note which is due to mature on March 18, 19____. The current balance is $9,000. The loan is collateralized by 9,000 bales of hay, 100 head of feeder pigs and 10 head of gilts. The interest due on the 18th will be $450.00, requiring a total payment of $9,450.

Due to the current circumstances, a renewal cannot be granted. The loan must be paid in full by March 18, 19____.

We hope the severe winter has not been unpleasant for you. Thank you for the opportunity to be of service.

Cordially,

CREDIT BUREAU RECORD ADJUSTMENT LETTER

LETTER G-19

An item greatly neglected by many banks: dismissal of suit filed. Correct the reported status of a customer's credit transaction.

XYZ Credit Bureau
Anytown, USA

Please update your credit files on Mr. _____. Previously, you had a report of suit filed by the ABC Bank in the amount of $2,560.00. Arrangements have been made by Mr. _____ to satisfy his obligations to the ABC Bank.

Please make any adjustment necessary on his credit bureau record, showing that the suit was dismissed pending an arrangement of satisfactory terms.

Cordially,

BANK'S LIMITED LIABILITY IN DEATH OF CUSTOMER LETTER

LETTER G-20

A tough personal situation developed when the bank was blamed for the death of a senior citizen who became despondent about the forthcoming foreclosure on a loan.

Dear _____:

Let me begin by apologizing for the delay in answering your questions concerning the death of _____. As I indicated in our telephone conversation, your letter must have been inadvertently misplaced by us.

It is reassuring to know that there are people such as yourself who believe that there is more to the situation than has been reported. Because Mr. _____ had refused to pay his loan, the bank was immediately blamed for his death. Needless to say, we are deeply concerned that all measures aimed at avoiding such a tragedy were not effective in this instance. The death was tragic, and no thinking person would deny it. I had hoped that the information from the coroner's report would have been released by now so that I could provide a more complete answer to your questions. Unfortunately, we are still awaiting the coroner's report.

The problem in Mr. _____ case was that he lived alone, and no one knew whether he was ill or not. I feel that this situation is a social problem, and not a matter limited to banking policies. But ABC Bank must share the responsibility with the community. In light of this tragedy, the bank is reviewing the "nonpayment policy" to find better ways to protect people unable to care for themselves.

Finally, let me say that society—all of us—must seek better ways to locate and assist people who need help. It will take the personal involvement of everyone to protect the sick and elderly. If lending institutions, neighbors and relatives work together then tragedies similar to Mr. _____ death can be eliminated. If you would care to discuss this matter further, please do not hesitate to call.

Kindest regards,

SYMPATHY ON LOSS OF A FRIEND

LETTER G-21

Always a difficult letter to write when a close friend dies.

Dear Mrs. _____:

Those of us who have had the distinct privilege of knowing your husband personally realize how empty our lives are by his death. What a loss to the community; but more, what a loss to you and to us who had received the warmth and emotions of John, helping to carry us through difficult situations.

He will be missed by all of us at the bank who cherished his wit and friendship.

You have my deepest sympathy in this time of loss.

Cordially,

SOLVING THE CREDIT LIFE INSURANCE PROBLEM LETTER

LETTER G-22

A change in the credit life program that affects banking customers.

Dear Credit Life Customer:

This is to notify you, our banking customer, that we now cover loans up to $20,000. Therefore, the new maximum charge for Credit Life Insurance will be $20.00; anything under that will be $1.00 per thousand.

The new rates will be effective as of April 20, 19____.

If at this time you do not have a loan with us, we hope you will keep this in mind in case you find need for a bank loan in the future.

If you have any questions about the new rates, please feel free to contact us at any time. We will be glad to answer your questions for you.

Sincerely,

BANK AS MUNICIPAL SECURITIES DEALER LETTER

LETTER G-23

Handling the municipal securities customer in compliance with the requirements of amendments to the Securities Exchange Act of 1934 that became effective in 1977.

Dear Securities Customer of ABC Bank:

As you may know, in 1975 Congress enacted amendments to the Securities Exchange Act of 1934 that provide for the regulation of municipal securities dealers such as the ABC Bank. This new regulation requires us to maintain additional information on our municipal securities customer accounts.

Since this regulation became effective on April 25, 1977, we must maintain in our files additional information from each customer of municipal securities. Please complete the enclosed form and return it to us in the addressed, prepaid envelope that we have provided for your convenience.

If you have any questions regarding the completion of this form, please contact your municipal securities representative at the bank. Your prompt reply is appreciated.

Cordially,

INTERNAL AUDIT EXAMINATION OF ACCOUNTS LETTER

LETTER G-24

This form letter is used to verify the account balances and eliminate any potential offset or dispute.

Dear Bank Customer:

Our *internal auditors* are making their regular examination of our accounts. With regard to that examination, your account has been selected for confirmation. Please compare the information stated below to your records as of 6/30/—.

Transactions since that date are not to be considered. If the information is not in agreement with your records, please state the difference on the reverse side of this letter and return it directly to our auditors in the envelope provided.

IF THE INFORMATION IS CORRECT, NO REPLY IS NECESSARY.

Balance outstanding from you is $———— on 6/30/—.

Please do not send payment to the auditors.

Very truly yours,

ABC Bank

CREDIT LIFE CLAIM LETTER

LETTER G-25

The difficult situation of requesting information for a death benefit claim from a customer of the bank.

Dear ————:

We want to express our sympathies for the loss of your husband on June 4. Your burden is understandable.

With the aid of credit life insurance, we may be able to assist in clearing up some indebtedness for which you and your husband wisely planned. We have enclosed several forms that your doctor can complete. Please sign the Proof of Claim form and attach a copy of the death certificate. Upon receipt of the above information, we will handle the processing of your credit life insurance claim.

Thank you for your cooperation in this matter and do not hesitate to call us if we can be of further service.

Cordially,

Eighteen Tough-minded Community Activity Letters

When called upon to become involved in a community activity, you are generally required to be persuasive in your approach to other people. Your success in this area of letter writing will result from *how* you approach the reader.

Community activities benefit a great many other people. Therefore, you will attempt to demonstrate how the reader, or someone in whom they have an interest, will benefit from accepting your persuasion. This group of letters provides a variety of community requests that will be required of you from time to time.

Capture reader interest with the first sentence. Use psychological appeals and reader benefits to convince the reader that the action requested or desired is of benefit to the *reader* in addition to the community. Letter H-2, for example is an excellent illustration of this plan of action in persuading business executives to volunteer for a community fund drive.

An interesting set of letters that can be useful, are the three letters presenting three different responses to the same situation request— political endorsements. Ready-to-use "Yes," "No," and neutral endorsement positions make this series of three letters valuable enough to be added to your letter portfolio.

LOCATING NEW BUSINESS FOR THE
COMMUNITY PROMOTION LETTER

LETTER H-1

This tough-minded, community-backed letter invites new industry and commercial business to locate in the area. The promotion was successful in bringing in new companies to a small community, that resulted in the development of 350 new jobs.

Dear _____:

In Anytown, Gateway to the Vacation Land, your best friend is the ABC Bank—with city services for industry in the friendly vacation setting.

Anytown—a great place to live and work, with ample facilities for fine living. No reason to ever leave Anytown—yet if you want more—metropolitan entertainment facilities are nearby.

We want you. Our reception and low tax rates, coupled with favorable financial programs, will prove that to you. Our community has a willing labor pool ready to go to work for you. Yes, we have a reserved place for your company in Anytown.

Community Assets:

- Junction point of two major railroads.
- Two major interstate highways.
- Approved airport facilities within five miles.
- Within one hour of major markets for your products and services.
- Hog, beef and dairy center.
- Adequate water, natural gas and fuel supplies.
- Factory buildings available.
- Active churches.
- Modern schools—adequate for future programs.
- Progressive and civic-minded business people.
- Outstanding recreational facilities.
- Forward-looking bank and financial services.
- And a lot of dedicated, hard-working, friendly people.

Call me at 222-2222 so I can send you more facts about our area.

This is an invitation to add your name to our growing list of Community assets.

Sincerely,

President

COMMUNITY LETTER—REQUEST FOR A VOLUNTEER

LETTER H-2

Persuading busy executives to give of their time for a community activity requires innovative appeals. This letter was successfully used to organize a fund drive.

Dear _____:

Little things mean a lot.

Don't you agree?

That's why I wanted to write you. As the chairman of the Children's Hospital Fund Drive, I think the little things you and I do for the community mean a lot. Even though I have a busy schedule here at the bank, I accepted the challenge of heading the Children's Fund Drive. But I need your help, so we can accomplish a successful fund raising that benefits the entire community.

You are a talented leader in the community. I personally need your help in organizing the fund drive in the industrial business sector. It may seem like a little thing to do—but it will mean a lot to the children who benefit from the fund drive.

On April 18, a small luncheon is planned for the fund drive captains at noon. If convenient for you, we'll all meet at my office at 11:30, then proceed to the restaurant where I have reserved a table just for the seven of us. I'll introduce you to the other drive captains when you arrive at my office. You know everyone, but a little mystery adds spice to an interesting planning session.

I look forward to your acceptance of this challenge.

Sincerely,

COMMUNITY ACTIVITY LETTER

LETTER H-3

An appeal to personal courage to get business people behind a community project. Most business people pride themselves (even if only secretly) on their personal courage.

Our city is filled with men and women who *WISH* something would happen. Only men and women of determination and purpose can *MAKE* things happen.

Which group do you belong to—the wishers or the makers?

If you have the courage to face facts—you will want to know who is responsible for the demise of the city's economic growth. Do you have the courage?

Knowing your determination, I'll tell you—it's YOU and I.

You will want to do something about the things that are NOT happening. You and I need to make an effort to support the Planning Commission in the forward approach to economic growth. It means:

- More jobs
- More business
- More growth

The "makers" in the past seized the opportunity to create our city. Now, you and I have the opportunity to capitalize on a courageous—yet controversial—economic program. Attend the meeting planned by the Growth Committee and support the future of our community.

Mark and mail the enclosed card so that we may count on your presence and support. Do it today.

Sincerely,

COMMUNITY LETTER

LETTER H-4

An appeal to a community drive—pledges that have not been fulfilled. Fair play is encouraged as you reach out for the charity of civic donations.

Dear _____:

Do you wonder if your contribution will be missed?

I am reminded of a small mining town in the old West that sought pledges from every family in the town, for the relief of a destitute family whose breadwinner was the victim of a mining disaster.

A large box was sealed and placed in one of the buildings where cash donations were to be dropped through a slot in the top of the box. When the townspeople gathered to open the box and present the destitute family with the donation, all were surprised that only one coin had been deposited in the box.

Each person thought, "My contribution will not be needed"; and therefore, nearly everyone had forgotten about his pledge.

A number of pledges, previously made, are still unfilled for the

_____ charity. Perhaps you have, for good reason, forgotten about the pledge. But your contribution is urgently needed.

Won't you send your contribution check today. It is missed by the _____ charity.

Sincerely,

HAPPINESS MEANS DONATIONS LETTER

LETTER H-5

A mass appeal to businesses needs a special touch to reach the executive.

Dear _____:

HOW MUCH IS YOUR CHILD'S
HAPPINESS WORTH TO YOU?

There are a lot of parents who cannot afford the cost of happiness . . . after a severe accident, or a burned arm or leg. That's why the Medical Center Drive which the ABC Bank willingly agreed to sponsor is so important to you and me.

The medical center undertakes treatment of children at no cost or a reduced cost, because the medical staff wants to use their skills to bring happiness back to the children who suffer.

But all this costs money. We need the support of every business person, so that the noble work of the skilled doctors can continue for the children.

I know how much your child's happiness is worth to you. Won't you please send a small part of that worth to us in the enclosed envelope? Then the medical center will be able to continue its work for the next unexpected child needing special care.

Sincerely,

ABC Bank
P.S. Your contribution is tax deductible.

PROMOTING A SALE FOR A COMMUNITY BENEFIT LETTER

LETTER H-6

Dear Business President:

As you have heard, the ABC Bank has been selling pens for the past two weeks; and we are happy to volunteer our marketing.

The funds from the open sale are to help your high school radio station in defraying the costs of educational radio broadcasting. The local radio station is supporting this promotion, also. Without seeking help from the fund raising project, the boys and girls at the high school cannot keep up with the high cost of broadcasting. As you know, educational radio operates without commercial sponsors.

We hope you will support the fund raising with the purchase of pens at a nominal cost of 50 cents each. The funds will be turned over to the high school radio station for purchase of records, public service material, and equipment required to stay on the air during the school year.

The pens are labeled with the High School name and radio station call letters. Perhaps you will want to order several dozen as customer and employee gifts. They are attractive and will make nice souvenirs.

Simply sign the enclosed card indicating the quantity you want, and a representative of the high school will deliver your pens. Yours in educational broadcasting,

ABC Bank

REFUSAL TO ACCEPT A COMMUNITY COMMITTEE APPOINTMENT LETTER

LETTER H-7

The best formula to refuse to accept a community appointment is to extend appreciation, give implied refusal and offer a suggested alternative replacement.

Dear _____:

The ABC Association has been a worthwhile activity for me. It offers a valuable business program. I appreciate your confidence expressed in nominating me as Chairman.

The position of Chairman is a demanding responsibility. The communications with other businesses require considerable time and effort to do the job properly. In light of my present obligations to the bank, I have given your nomination considerable thought. Mary and I have discussed this unique honor. Even though she is willing to undergo the sacrifice of my being involved in another activity, I do not feel further time from the family would be fair to them or me. The position of Chairman would be better filled by someone else during the coming year.

Perhaps you would want to consider John Marshall for the position of Chairman. He is unmarried and established in his own business. John would be an enthusiastic Chairman. I am sure he will be capable of adding new spark to the Association.

You have my best wishes in locating the right candidate for the most important position of Chairman.

Cordially,

PERSUASIVE REQUEST FOR A SPEAKER LETTER

LETTER H-8

A partial letter to the speaker stating the essential details of the speech, while stressing a key benefit of the speaker's need to help the community.

Our banquet will be held at the DEF Hotel, Friday, June 28, at 8 p.m. You will enjoy the dinner and planned program. I will see that you are picked up at the airport and returned that evening or the next morning, depending upon your preference. Of course, you will be reimbursed for your traveling and overnight hotel expenses, which will give you an opportunity to visit with us if your schedule allows. The 150 persons expected to attend would be happy to discuss your subject material further, after the banquet. Certainly, the twenty minutes allotted the speaker will only excite the avid interest of those in attendance who are all interested in listening to your expert discussion. We feel your views will greatly aid our community. There has been much interest in learning how you put the new program into effect last year.

BANK SUPPORT OF FINE ART LETTER

LETTER H-9

Banks are becoming more involved with projects to fulfill the corporate requirements for better community relationships.

Dear Neighbor:

This month, the ABC Bank will open the Bank's Gallery of Fine Art. You are invited to attend the special preview on September 20th.

During the past year, the ABC Bank has obtained almost $180,000 worth of art, thanks to a community grant of $25,000 and matching funds from the bank and community leaders. On loan from major galleries around the world are special Fine Art works that will be on display in the Bank Gallery of Fine Art.

The work on display this month contains examples of artists who have made major contributions to the development of fine art during the 19th century. The collection represents 35 major artists of world fame.

We are pleased to open this gallery in order to provide the community with a vital extension to the world of fine arts. We hope it will provide you with a regional resource to enrich your awareness of world-wide fine art masters.

You and your family are invited to the preview on September 20th at the bank's art gallery, just off the main lobby. Stop by and enjoy the day with us.

Cordially,

"THANKS FOR VOLUNTEERING" LETTER

LETTER H-10

To ensure continued support for future community drives, a well-designed success letter is needed.

Dear Volunteer:

Thousands of volunteers such as you, guaranteed the success of the Community Drive campaign for 19____. Total contributions exceeded last year's total by 27%. During the campaign, you encouraged friends and neighbors to donate $145,743—for the best year ever!

This means new services for our community, including the ambulance rescue service so badly needed for unexpected crises.

Volunteers are the key to the success of the community drive. Our expenses are less than 1% of the donations, allowing more funds to be used by the community. Also, whenever you see the new rescue service in operation, someone will be saying, again, "Thank you for what you did in 19____."

Sincerely,

SAYING "NO" TO THE POLITICAL ENDORSEMENT LETTER

LETTER H-11

A partial letter that keeps the bank and the banker out of the political arena, without losing the political support of a potential future elected official.

Political endorsements such as you have requested, require the bank's Board of Directors' approval. As you are probably aware, the Board of Directors is not scheduling a meeting until close to the election date. Since the endorsement decision will be too late to be useful in your campaign, we will not be in a position to present your request to the board.

It is with regret that we are unable to publicly "endorse" your candidacy for Commissioner. You are a fine and capable campaigner. Our inability to add our endorsement to your upcoming election should not reduce your total votes at the polls in November.

SAYING "YES" TO THE POLITICAL ENDORSEMENT LETTER

LETTER H-12

A partial letter to acknowledge the bank's firm support behind an incumbent office holder.

With the approval of the Board of Directors, we are delighted to once again support your re-election to the Judgeship. Your long record of outstanding service to the community speaks for itself. We add our endorsement to the long list of your supporters.

THE NEUTRAL POLITICAL POLICY LETTER

LETTER H-13

A partial letter that states a neutral position between two candidates without offending either.

It is seldom that our community has aspiring to the same office, two outstanding people whom the bank wishes could both be winners at the November polls. This unique dilemma has resulted in an equal "vote of confidence" for both candidates by the management staff at the ABC Bank.

It is our desire to encourage both candidates to campaign hard. Both are deserving of election and we know it will be a difficult choice for voters. The real winner, of course, will be the community, when two of the finest choose to dedicate themselves to public service. Regardless of the final results in November, we wish the very best for each candidate.

GROUP CHARITY GIFT LETTER

LETTER H-14

An appeal to a company or group for charitable gifts.

Dear Friends:

May I ask a favor of you—the kind of favor I would not mind if I were in your place? When one of your company workers dies from _____, why not give funds to the Community Fund Drive as a "Living Remembrance?"

Gifts are greatly needed for continuous programs of research, education and services to patients. The contributions, of course, are tax deductible. The Community Fund will acknowledge all group gifts. Also, a special memorial card is sent to the family of the deceased.

The enclosed packet, being sent as the bank's small part in defraying contribution expense, has envelopes, cards and a group collection. The Fund Drive will also send to the company giving the "Living Remembrance" a special letter of acknowledgment.

Will you help us to help you and your employees? It will be greatly appreciated.

Sincerely,

OFFERING HELP AFTER A MAJOR DISASTER LETTER

LETTER H-15

Sympathy with offer of banking assistance following a disaster.

Dear _____:

After viewing the extensive damage to your business, we want to express our sympathy to you and your employees. We realize that discontinuing business for repairs will be costly.

The bank has available a vacant building that you can use for temporary offices, or storage of machinery and equipment. It is yours to use as our guest.

If we can be of assistance in extending the facilities of our bank, please call me.

Sincerely,

COMMUNITY PROGRESS LETTER

LETTER H-16

A partial letter that builds for the community future.

The completion of one major expansion and the start of another, highlighted the county activities during the past year. While the ABC Company was beginning production of industrial parts for the copper mining industry in a new 12 million dollar plant, the city of Anytown was moving forward with a 5 million dollar plant expansion project for industrial motor production. The use of tax abatements and tax incentives has enabled the community to benefit from an increase of 7,200 industrial jobs. Also, the industrial job increase benefits other businesses—more shopping areas, more residential construction, more restaurants and a new elementary school—resulting in an additional 7,450 service-related jobs.

The ABC Bank is proud to be part of the planning that allows our city to build for a more stable future.

SAYING "YES" TO A COMMUNITY
MASTER PLAN COMMITTEE LETTER

LETTER H-17

A partial letter to accept a beneficial community assignment.

The resources of the ABC Bank fully support the long-range planning to be undertaken in establishing a county-wide Master Plan for the community's future growth.

We will participate in any committee assignments as requested. The financial experience of our senior bank officers is at the disposal of the Master Plan Committee. The future of the community and the ABC Bank are closely related. It is our desire to build a stronger and more beautiful community as a heritage for future citizens of the county.

SUPPORT FOR THE NEW LIBRARY BUILDING PROGRAM LETTER

LETTER H-18

A partial letter that encourages public support for a new library building.

The services of the County Public Library are used by more individuals than any other public service available. The wisdom of the ages and the science of tomorrow are under the guardianship of our public library. Precious knowledge is available to all of our community residents. Knowledge that can improve our skills and make us more productive and wholesome reading entertainment are available on the library shelves.

The ABC Bank supports the county plans to build the new library building at the corner of Main and 10th Street. Although the cost of the building has become a subject of discussion, we feel that the program will be a great benefit to all the people in the community. Each and every one of us will profit by the added library facility.

GROUP *I* LETTERS

Nineteen Specially Selected Employee Relations Letters That Answer Every Major Situation and Increase Banking Morale

Letters to the banking staff are important builders of the bank's important intangible asset—high morale!

This group of specially selected employee relations letters covers every major staff situation; from the birth of a child to the death of an employee. Letters on resigning, promotions and new staff employee starts are packed into this unique group of internal letters. Good communications dispel employee rumors, and you will find several excellent letters specifically for that purpose.

Read this entire group of letters and you will probably find, as we did; that if one bank used all these letters consistently, it would be a great bank for which to work.

PROFIT-ORIENTED EMPLOYEE RELATIONS LETTER

LETTER I-1

A tough-minded employee relations memo that boosts morale, states the profit problem and dispels rumors of layoffs.

ALL OFFICERS AND SUPERVISORS:

As you have read, our first quarter net income was up ____%
over the comparable three months of 19____.

This is a creditable showing; especially in view of the enormous
pressures on the profit margins of larger banks, because of the
high cost of money-market funds. Our own profit margin—that
is, our net income for the quarter is a percentage of gross
revenues—dropped from last year's ____% to ____%.

This trend sharply underscores the continuing need for holding
down costs wherever we can, if we are to achieve our goal of
becoming the city's most profitable bank.

Over the past few weeks, I think that all of you have done an
outstanding job of ferreting out places in your areas where
budget cuts could be made without seriously interfering with the
achievement of major objectives. Through your conscientious
cooperation, substantial reductions have been made in
_____ Bank's over-all budget for the year.

What's more, these economies have been effected without re-
leasing a single staff member. Nor do we have any plans for
such releases in the future.

I appreciate the commendable spirit you have shown in this
effort to hold down costs and I am confident that as a result, we
can look forward to a more productive and profitable year.

President

"YOU'RE THE GREATEST" BANK/STAFF LETTER

LETTER I-2

Year-end analysis of the banking situation.

Dear Bank Staff and Officers:

As we approach the end of another calendar year, I have
paused to reflect on the high caliber men and women that
change this bank from one of marble and stone to one of a
dynamic living organization. It is your loyal cooperation that
caused this bank to become a trusted, stable anchor in this city.

During the past year of economic re-adjustment in our community, we have heard much talk of gloom and doom, loss of
population and business downturn. But it has been your positive mental attitude that has allowed your bank to grow and
prosper during the toughest time this country has seen since
the end of the second World War. We can look forward with
enthusiasm to personal prosperity and continued success at
the bank.

Our own economic forecast for the coming year is bright—both for us and for the community. New opportunities are opening up each month for those who demonstrate leadership qualities. I want all of you to share in the continued progress and financial strength demonstrated during the past year.

Your creative talent is needed on the day-to-day details of your own job. Look at each transaction and each problem as an opportunity to find a better—even *easier* way to do your job. It is up to you to find a way to top the success of the year just closing.

Sincerely,

President

AN EMPLOYEE BOOSTER THAT SAYS, "PASS IT ON!" LETTER

LETTER I-3

Year-end work gets hectic and bank lines get longer. An ideal time to boost bank employee morale, with a unique twist that explains how they contribute to the happiness of their customers.

Dear Staff:

CHRISTMAS BRINGS SOME HIDDEN JOYS!

Banking has its ups and downs, but at this time of the year we all have an opportunity to bring some hidden joy to nearly every family in our valley. As we double our work pace to approve hurry-up loans, close old Christmas Club Accounts and re-open new ones, cash payroll checks or handle savings transactions, you and I have an opportunity to light the candle of happiness.

It is within your own unique power as you meet each customer face-to-face, to create a Christmas Spirit—hope for a discouraged person.

Just a friendly smile, or word from you and me will make this Christmas a most joyous one. Certainly, it will boost our spirit as giver, as well as the customer needing inspiration from our friendly smile. We may never know who desperately needs the hidden joy of our friendly inspiration during this Christmas rush.

It is my wish that we maintain the joy of the Christmas Spirit every day of the coming year.

Sincerely,

President

"CHATTER"—ON RESIGNING LETTER

LETTER I-4

A letter to keep a valuable bank employee that is planning to resign because a pay raise request was turned down.

Dear _____:

I cannot let your contemplated resignation be put on paper by you without some "chatter" from me. You have been part of my team for a long time. But you will never be an "old shoe" even though you did not get the raise in pay that you requested.

You and I both know that expenses have been a "hot" subject here at the bank during the past year. To the board, a pay raise is an expense. Many salary increases were rejected this year. I'll not kid you—some officers did get increases. Mostly, the situations were unique or overdue promises. I can understand your thoughts, too. Your request was real and deserving from your point of view. Don't get the idea the bank believes that you have not made a valuable contribution to our division's progress. You have.

Now, as to your contemplated resignation, (*name*), that's strictly up to you. It's your future—you and your family's. What I want to say is—I'd like you to stay if *you* can live under the stress of doing an excellent job, as usual, without receiving immediate monetary rewards.

Personally, I think this bank is good for you and you are good for this bank. You will find as you grow older that some non-monetary rewards are far greater than immediate cash in the working world. I didn't believe it either when I was your age.

So, (*name*), I will be out of town for a few days. But I look forward to *not* seeing your resignation letter when I return.

Best wishes,

Senior Vice-President

ON RESIGNING—WITH HELP OUT THE DOOR LETTER

LETTER I-5

The letter that helps get rid of the "dead wood" found in any organization.

Dear _____:

I cannot let your comment concerning "resignation" become official without reviewing your bank progress.

You have served this bank well in the five years that you have been "aboard." Of course, a few officers have advanced at a faster pace, but that is no reflection on your ability. You are an excellent lending officer.

Should you decide to formally resign, you will have my continued support for future success at any bank position accepted by you. Frankly, I believe your talent should lead you to the top in banking circles. It is unfortunate that some must choose to change banks in order to further a career. Of course, I would prefer that you stay as a member of my management team.

Regardless of your ultimate decision in furthering your personal growth, it will not stand in the way of our friendship.

Sincerely,

Vice-President

RESIGNATION OF A CLOSE FRIEND AND KEY EXECUTIVE LETTER

LETTER I-6

Mandatory retirement after many years of service needs a special message.

Dear _____:

My thoughts are split as I realize your resignation as Vice-President is official next Friday. You have greatly contributed to the reputation of the ABC Bank during your thirty years of faithful service to the bank and to the community. For this, you have my admiration and friendship.

It will be difficult to think of the bank without your steady leadership. I will always have a feeling of loss whenever I walk into your old office. We have seen some great changes in the banking business and solved some difficult problems over your mahogany desk.

I wish you a future of great happiness. Now you can pursue those inner dreams you had to defer under the pressure of heavy work obligations. Of course, there is no greater pleasure than to pause after thirty years to review your many accomplishments. I also take note of the many friends you have made during the past years.

Old friend, I wish you many more pleasant years. Certainly, your reward is well-deserved for all you have done for the bank and the community.

Sincerely,

President

EMPLOYEE RELATIONS—PROMOTION ANNOUNCEMENT LETTER

LETTER I-7

Always look for an opportunity to recognize success in your employees. Even though you personally congratulate an employee on a promotion, send a written letter. A great boost in morale—and performance—will be noticed.

Dear _____:

Congratulations on your promotion.

The bank's Board of Directors officially named you a Vice President effective _____.

My personal note of thanks goes along with your new title as you assume additional responsibility in the style of your successful past performance.

Sincerely,

President

PROMOTION CONGRATULATIONS TO A BANK STAFF MEMBER LETTER

LETTER I-8

A written note to a subordinate staff member from a bank officer is in order for morale building and business friendships that count.

Dear _____:

The announcement of your step up the ladder now makes it official. There is no doubt in my mind that your promotion was well-deserved.

I am sorry to lose you to another unit of the bank, but I know all of us benefit because of your abilities.

You have my congratulations and wishes for the best of luck.

Sincerely,

Treasurer

PROMOTION—CONGRATULATIONS LETTER

LETTER I-9

A letter of congratulations on a staff promotion no matter how minor, will improve morale and tell the staffer that you are interested in his personal welfare.

Dear _____:

It is always a delight to be able to say, "Thank you—for a job well done!"

That is exactly what we meant when you were promoted to Assistant Treasurer. Your enthusiasm and dedication to your work is a mark of your accomplishments. Always maintain these secret keys to your career success. Surely, they will aid you in your personal happiness.

All of us at the bank wish you good fortune in your new responsibilities.

Cordially,

EMPLOYEE RELATIONS—A NEW BIRTH LETTER

LETTER I-10

Major events in the lives of employees offer natural opportunities to let them know you are interested.

Dear _____:

The birth of your daughter/son, (name), was certainly a special event for you and your wife, (name). I know how proud both of you are in announcing (name) birth.

As she/he grows she'll/he'll be a complex individual. Someone to worry about, someone to care for, someone to be proud of and someone with whom to share happiness.

I want to add my good wishes for your daughter's/son's bright and happy future. The small gift from the bank is a memento of the happy occasion.

You and your wife have my congratulations.

Very truly yours,

Senior Vice-President

CONGRATULATIONS ON MARRIAGE PLANS LETTER

LETTER I-11

A time of happiness—The *most* important decision in every person's life. After all, it sets the trend and bends the path of the future, permanently.

Dear _____:

We were delighted to hear that you have set your heart in happiness. Congratulations on your forthcoming marriage.

Your associates at the bank send their best wishes for your future happiness. I had the pleasure of shopping for a special gift that you and your bride/groom will really cherish in your future years together.

Knowing your plans as a member of the bank's staff, I think the selection is just right. It is on the way with our best wishes.

Sincerely,

DEATH OF EMPLOYEE LETTER

LETTER I-12

One of the most difficult letters to write when you must express sympathy to the widow or widower of an employee. Stress the good qualities and why you will miss the person.

Dear _____:

The passing of _____ comes as an untimely shock that has saddened all of his associates at the bank.

We shall remember him as a conscientious, dedicated member of our staff. He was pleasant, well-liked, and his presence made all our lives happier.

You and your family have our sincere condolences.

ABC Bank

Vice-President

WELCOME TO A NEW EMPLOYEE LETTER

LETTER I-13

A letter of welcome is important—to ease the tension of the first difficult days as a new bank employee. This may be one of the most important morale-builders for the new employee.

Dear _____:

You are now a very important part of the ABC Bank.

As President, I extend a hearty welcome and hope you will enjoy being a part of the ABC team. I know your first day is difficult; remembering new faces and procedures. The first day on my first job reminds me that things will seem strange, and the work more difficult than it really is.

Even though you are new to the bank, I know you are going to enjoy your work here. The ABC Bank is the best in the city and that is something you can share with pride. We work as a team and everyone will be willing to help you succeed.

Congratulations on choosing to join the best bank. I know you will give your best, and in return you can expect the best in benefits from us.

Sincerely,

President

BRANCH BANK NEW STAFF WELCOME LETTER

LETTER I-14

Welcome into a large organization with multiple bank branches eliminates organization problems.

Dear Mr. _____:

It is a genuine pleasure to welcome you into the ABC Bank organization as a member of the Northside Branch.

I hope you and I will have a chance to become personally acquainted before long. However, there are some thoughts I would like to convey to you right now, as you are starting your ABC Bank career.

The fact that you have been selected as an ABC Bank representative from a large number of candidates, indicates you possess the basic qualifications for success in banking and that you are the high caliber type of individual we are proud to have in our organization. You have reason to be proud, too, of the bank you have chosen.

Opportunities in a growing bank, such as ABC Bank, are unlimited for those who are willing to work hard and make the most of their talents and abilities. We will expect a great deal of effort on your part, and we are prepared to help you reach the goal you have set for yourself.

You can be sure we will be following your progress with interest, and that all management will want to assist you in every way possible to make your career with ABC Bank a success.

We are happy to welcome you as a member of the ABC Bank staff.

Cordially,

President

WELCOME TO A NEW BANK OFFICER LETTER

LETTER I-15

Letter of welcome to an experienced career banker joining your bank.

Dear _____:

Welcome to the ABC Bank!

It is with great pride that we are announcing your decision to join our banking staff as Assistant Vice-President.

We know you will find many challenges and opportunities that will benefit the bank and you. Your new responsibilities are an important part of our bank's service. We know you will find ways to improve our banking position in the community. Your past record speaks of that fact.

I look forward to your input as the newest team member of our management staff. Best wishes for a successful and bright future with ABC Bank.

Sincerely,

WELCOME TO A NEW BANK STAFF MEMBER LETTER

LETTER I-16

Letter of welcome to an experienced employee joining the staff.

Dear _____:

It is a pleasure, Mr. _____ . . .
To welcome you as a new member of the ABC Bank staff.

Since 1914, the ABC Bank has built a reputation of having the finest employees to serve the community. We are proud of the men and women who carry forward this reputation. Now, you are part of this fine staff.

I shall do everything I can to merit your confidence in your new career decision. I look forward to a long and pleasant relationship as you progress with the bank.

Sincerely,

EMPLOYEE RELOCATION PARAGRAPH

LETTER I-17

Good bank employees are hard to find. A special paragraph for temporary financial assistance in acquiring a new home on relocation, needs to be clearly defined.

Should you require financial assistance in purchasing a home on relocating in the area, the bank will consider granting a loan for a period not to exceed twelve months in an amount equal to the necessary down-payment on a new home or the amount of equity in your present property; whichever is less. Your equity in the present property represents the difference between the Current Fair Market Price and all outstanding mortgages and liens on the property.

PROFIT-SHARING BENEFIT LETTER

LETTER I-18

A partial letter that praises the bank staff for their contribution to the profit-sharing plan.

The bank's matching share of the profit-sharing plan for 19____ was the highest reward that the Board of Directors had the pleasure to approve. The value of this year's contribution was a direct result of your successful performance.

The search for better service to our customers is measured by the improved income each year. As a result of better service, we can look forward to ever-increasing contributions to your profit-sharing plan in the future.

STAFF SUGGESTION "THANK YOU" LETTER

LETTER I-19

A partial letter that expresses appreciation for a worthwhile suggestion.

Your suggestion is being prepared for formal introduction into the ABC Bank's operations procedure. We appreciate the time and thought you have given to this innovative suggestion.

You have made an outstanding contribution to improve customer service. Mr. _____, Vice-President of Operations joins me in expressing our sincere thanks.

GROUP *J* LETTERS

Twenty-nine Innovative
Stockholder Letters

Stockholders are generally a cautious group of individuals. To the bank, stockholders are both investors and customers. This double role is important to remember in preparing messages to this special group of people.

The stockholder letter must respond to the investment benefits and also to the customer benefits, in order to present a complete message. In the following group of letters, this double benefit to the reader is evident. Bank stockholders want a good return on their investment, but conservative stability and safety of the investment are more important. Banking letters to stockholders strongly stress these factors.

Many banks offer new services, such as bank cards, to the stockholder group first. Several letters in this group are for this purpose, which is an excellent way to maintain the best in stockholder-bank relationships.

Personal letters are included that welcome a new stockholder or express the goodwill of the bank on the "loss" of a stockholder. Also, letters to explain the solidarity of the bank or future plans are included in this group.

ANNOUNCING TOTAL NEW BANK MANAGEMENT LETTER

LETTER J-1

An effective letter used by a small bank to announce the change of senior management and offer to buy minority stock holdings if anyone is dissatisfied.

To ALL STOCKHOLDERS:

This is to announce that Jeffrey _____ and William _____ have purchased the control of the _____ State Bank from Edgar _____, effective September 21, 19___.

In order to justify the capital investment and to maintain two additional business-oriented officers to better serve the community, it may be difficult to maintain the dividend structure to which you have become accustomed.

For your consideration, we are tendering an offer good through October 20, 19___, of $300.00 per share for any shares of minority stock you may wish to sell. The offer will terminate on October 20, 19___ at midnight.

Enclosed is a proxy for a special meeting of the stockholders which is called for 3:00 P.M. October 14, 19___ at the offices of the bank. You are invited to attend, but if unable, please sign the enclosed proxy card and mail it prior to October 10, 19___.

Your interest in good banking is appreciated.

Sincerely yours,

Chairman of the Board

SPECIAL MEETING STOCKHOLDERS LETTER

LETTER J-2

TO THE STOCKHOLDERS:

You are hereby notified that a Special Meeting of the Stockholders of the ABC Bank, will be held in the Upstairs Meeting Room of the banking house, at 7:00 P.M. on Monday, the 11th day of June, 19___; for the purpose of considering and voting on the following special matter to be submitted to the stockholders:

1. A resolution which has been prepared and which may be examined at any time during office hours prior to the aforesaid meeting providing for:

   An amendment to the Charter of Incorporation to authorize an increase in the capital stock of the bank from $200,000 to $233,750.

2. To transact all such other business pertinent to the above, as may come before the meeting.

If you are unable to attend, please execute the attached proxy and return it promptly.

Cordially,

NEW STOCK SUBSCRIPTION FOR STOCKHOLDERS LETTER

LETTER J-3

Dear Stockholder:

Enclosed is your Certificate showing the number of 30-day, transferable stock rights due you under the proposal to increase the capital stock of the bank that was accepted by the stockholders at the Special Meeting held June 11, 19____. We are also enclosing, for your use, a STOCK SUBSCRIPTION FORM and several ASSIGNMENT OF STOCK RIGHTS forms.

Your rights are good for a period of thirty (30) days from the date of issuance. They will expire at 12:00 noon, Wednesday, July 11, 19____. During the 30-day period, you can exchange your rights for new shares of $10.00 par value capital stock of the bank. The exchange rate will be one (1) new share of stock for each sixteen (16) rights surrendered for exchange and accompanied by a $70.00 cash payment.

To subscribe to new shares, you must use a STOCK SUB-SCRIPTION FORM. We are enclosing a form for your use. Additional forms may be picked up at the bank. Be sure that you complete the STOCK SUBSCRIPTION FORM as follows:

1. Show the number of shares to which you subscribe.
2. Show the total number of stock rights you are presenting for exchange.
3. Show the total cash payment enclosed with your subscription.
4. Show the name and complete address of the person to whom the new shares of stock are to be issued.
5. Show the Social Security number of the person to whom the new shares are to be issued. *No subscription form will be accepted without the proper Social Security number.*
6. Attach to the completed Subscription Form the:
   a. Correct number of Rights Certificates and/or Rights Assignment forms for the number of shares you are requesting (16 rights per share).
   b. Correct total cash payment for the number of shares you are requesting ($70.00 per share).
   Example: If you wish to purchase 10 new shares, you will need to surrender a total of 160 rights (16 × 10 new shares) and your total cash payment of $700.00 ($70.00 × 10 new shares).

These rights are transferable. During the 30-day period, it will be possible for you to acquire sufficient additional rights to complete the number necessary for a share of stock. By the same token, you can also dispose of any excess rights that you have. For your use in the acquiring or disposing of rights, we are enclosing several ASSIGNMENT OF STOCK RIGHTS forms. All transfers of rights must be made between individuals. The bank will not act as agent for any transfer of rights.

No fractional shares of stock will be issued. At the end of the 30-day period (12:00 noon, Wednesday, July 11, 19____), all unsurrendered rights will expire, and the holders of such unsur-rendered rights will be paid $4.375 for each right still held. The holder of unsurrendered rights will, for payment purposes, be considered to be the stockholder to whom the rights are origi-nally issued; unless the bank has been notified in writing by use of an ASSIGNMENT OF STOCK RIGHTS form filed with the bank prior to the date of expiration of the stock rights (12:00 noon, Wednesday, July 11, 19____).

Additional SUBSCRIPTION FORMS and additional ASSIGN-MENT OF STOCK RIGHTS forms may be picked up at the bank.

We will be glad to answer any questions that you may have.

Yours very truly,

Executive Vice-President

COST OF FUNDS PROBLEM STOCKHOLDERS LETTER

LETTER J-4

FELLOW STOCKHOLDERS:

I am pleased to report that 19____ was a good year for _____ Bank. It was achieved while the bank officials worked vigorously to solve the problems arising from the in-creased cost of funds.

Continued improvement in the overall financial strength of the Bank were the highlights of 19____.

The _____ Bank is playing an important role in making _____ City a better place to work and invest. Our opera-tions have a beneficial effect on positive growth within our state.

Our prime objectives, as detailed in the enclosed report, are to continue to work for a solution to the cost of funds problem and to improve the profit margins as customer service is improved.

We are strongly committed to an enlarged retail banking program as we move forward into next year.

Sincerely,

Chairman of the Board

SPECIAL SERVICE FOR STOCKHOLDERS LETTER
LETTER J-5

Dear Shareholder:

ABC Bank's newest service is our credit card, the most widely used and accepted bank card in the world. As a Stockholder of our bank, I would like to personally invite you to be among the first to take advantage of the benefits available to you with ABC's credit card. Among them, an interest-free purchase account when the 25-day repayment option is utilized, purchasing power at nearly 2,000,000 stores and businesses around the world, and the availability of emergency funds at 20,000 affiliated banks. Your card will be instantly accepted whether you shop in person, by mail, or phone. In addition, your purchases may be consolidated into one monthly bill, saving you time and money.

Even if you are presently enjoying the convenience of a bank card, we hope that you will accept our card.

Should you desire to do so, please return this letter with your signature and then "relax" with an ABC Bank Card.

Very truly yours,

President

DIVIDEND INCREASE STOCKHOLDER'S LETTER
LETTER J-6

Solid growth of the bank is highlighted.

Dear Shareholder:

The year ending _____, 19___, was one of solid achievement for the ABC Bank in continuing to serve the banking needs of its customers and earning an adequate return for its shareholders.

Net income for the year was $_____ or $_____ per share, as compared with $_____ or $_____ per share for the previous year. These improved earnings reflect the strength of our loan portfolio.

In December, 19___, the bank's annual dividend rate was raised by ___ cents per share, an increase of ___%. Dividends have now been raised in three consecutive years and in twelve of the last nineteen years. As a result of this most recent increase, the dividend rate now stands at ___ cents per year.

At the end of another successful year, we wish to express appreciation for the fine performance of the banking staff. We are fortunate to have employees of exceptional ability, which speaks well for the bank's future.

Sincerely,

Chairman and President

LOSS OF STOCKHOLDER LETTER

LETTER J-7

An expression of goodwill is a well-written letter to a "lost" stockholder.

Dear _____:

As a bank with several hundred stockholders, many of them neighbors and friends, I see new names appear occasionally. But when the name of a former stockholder of ABC Bank is dropped, I am always disappointed.

Perhaps you changed addresses or transferred the stock to another member of your family. Whatever the reason, we at ABC Bank hope to retain your friendship and goodwill.

Should there be any reason for your discontinuing stock ownership due to bank policies, please drop me a note. It is always our policy to maintain the "friendliest" bank relations with our customers and stockholders.

Yours for better banking.

Cordially,

ABC Bank
Chairman of the Board

WELCOME TO NEW STOCKHOLDER LETTER

LETTER J-8

New stockholders should receive a welcome from the bank.

Dear _____:

The Board of Directors of the ABC Bank extends a welcome to you as a stockholder.

We will send you regular reports on earnings and bank progress in addition to the annual report.

The ABC Bank has assets of $_____ million, and 41 employees whom we count as assets, too. The bank is growing with *10,000* Demand Deposit accounts, *15,000* savings accounts, and *3,000* commercial and personal loans and mortgages. The ABC Bank serves a wonderful community and is showing steady growth.

The Board and I invite you to contribute any suggestions you may have for better banking.

Sincerely,

Chairman of the Board

REQUEST FOR STOCKHOLDER PROXY LETTER

LETTER J-9

A reminder to major bank stockholders for a return of the proxy.

Dear Stockholder:

As of today, we have not received a proxy from you for the Special Stockholders Meeting to be held October 14, 19___.

Accept our thanks and disregard this request if you have already mailed your proxy.

However, if you have not returned your proxy or are not certain whether you did, please complete the enclosed proxy form. If you do not expect to vote directly at the meeting, we want you to be represented. Please mail your proxy today in the enclosed reply envelope.

Cordially,

OVERDRAFT CHECKING FOR STOCKHOLDERS LETTER

LETTER J-10

Offer new banking services to stockholders for big bank dividends.

Dear ABC Bank Stockholder:

CASH CUSHION CHECKING is an entirely new banking service being offered by your bank. It lets you write a check bigger than the balance in your checking account. When your check is presented for payment, funds are automatically transferred in increments of $100 from your established CASH CUSHION to your checking account.

The automatic transfers become loans to you and, as you repay, the principal amount of your cash reserve—CASH CUSHION—becomes available to you for use again and again.

If you would like to have the CASH CUSHION CHECKING privilege established for you, simply sign the enclosed card and return it to the bank in the prepaid envelope. As one of our stockholders, we want you to be one of the first to have access to ABC Bank's new banking service.

Sincerely yours,

ANNUAL STOCKHOLDER'S NOTICE WITH PROXY LETTER

LETTER J-11

Dear _____:

Please be advised that the annual meeting of the stockholders of the ABC Bank, will be held Thursday, July 14, 19____, at the office of the bank at 1:00 P.M.

The purpose of the meeting is to elect five (5) directors and transact any other business that may come before the meeting.

If you are unable to be present at this meeting, please sign and return the lower portion of this letter which will serve as your proxy.

Very truly yours,

President

PROXY

I hereby appoint _____ as my Attorney and Agent, to vote as my Proxy at the July 14, 19____, annual stockholders meeting of ABC Bank; according to the number of votes I should be entitled to vote if personally present, with power of substitution.

In witness whereof, I have hereunto set my hand and seal this _____ day of _____ A.D., 19____.

In presence of:

_____
Stockholder's Signature

_____
Witness

_____
Social Security Number

REPORT ON OPERATIONS TO STOCKHOLDER LETTER

LETTER J-12

Dear Stockholder:

Net income for the first two quarters ending June 30, 19____, totaled $2.02 per share as compared to $1.90 per share earned for a like period in 19____. This represents an increase of 6%.

We have seen substantial earnings improvement the last two months as a result of some adjustments made at the end of the first quarter. We expect this trend to continue, and are confident that we will be able to meet the earnings projections of 19____.

Deposits are up approximately $31,000,000, an increase of 22%. This is the largest deposit increase your holding company has experienced in any one-year period.

We look forward to the beginning of the construction of the new bank building. Also, we expect to receive regulatory approval on the application to acquire the XYZ Bank, sometime during the third quarter.

We are grateful for the continued loyalty and support of our stockholders and customers.

Sincerely,

Chairman of the Board and President

MEASUREMENT OF SAFETY STOCKHOLDER'S LETTER

LETTER J-13

A partial letter that directs attention to the Capital Adequacy Ratio, Liquidity Ratio and Net Interest Income Ratio.

The result of management decisions has given the bank a high degree of liquidity which is sufficient to meet the increasing loan demands that we forecast for the next five years. The widely accepted measure of safety, the Capital Adequacy Ratio, reflects our position. The average total capital divided by the average total assets, shows that we have been successful in meeting our goal above the 7% level for this important ratio.

The bank is above the national banking system's average for the Liquidity Ratio, which is another measurement of safety. This is a ratio of cash and readily marketable assets to deposits. The impact on earnings from maintaining the measures of safety is reflected in the ratio of Net Interest Income dividend by Earning Assets. Earnings tend to decline when the interest rates for loans and securities are low. The bank is attempting to balance the interest-sensitive assets and liabilities in order to stabilize the fluctuation in earnings.

PEOPLE AS A SOURCE OF STRENGTH STOCKHOLDER'S LETTER

LETTER J-14

A partial letter that personalizes the banking services.

The dedication and competence of the men and women of the ABC Bank is a source of pride to us, making possible the bank's outstanding performance last year. These efforts were particularly noteworthy during the current winter—a period of crisis for the nation. The personal performance of our staff allows us to offer a unique service while being a bank of modest size. The welfare of thousands of banking customers was of primary importance to our staff. Our efforts in the coming year are devoted to that friendly and personal service objective.

COMPUTERIZED DATA BANK FOR STOCKHOLDERS LETTER

LETTER J-15

A partial letter that explains the computer strength of information available to customers and stockholders.

Also available to business clients or to our stockholders, is the information contained in our computerized data bank for each of the 43 communities in our seven-county service area. The ABC Bank's computer analyzes over 1,000 factors affecting investment and plant location needs. We are able to quickly match business requirements to our service area for business consideration.

PROBLEMS OF RECESSION AND INFLATION LETTER

LETTER J-16

A partial stockholders letter that explains the effect of recession and inflation on the bank.

> The deepening recession continues to take its toll, resulting in a higher level of loan losses. In addition, inflationary factors cause an increase in our cost of doing business. For these reasons, the increase in profits generated in the third and fourth quarters were not of the magnitude of those achieved in the second quarter. Our outlook for the economy leads us to expect this downward trend to continue during the first half of next year.

BANKING STRENGTH IN BRANCHES—STOCKHOLDERS LETTER

LETTER J-17

A partial letter explaining the strength of branch banking.

> Our stockholders will be pleased to learn that the growing network of bank branches have helped build and strengthen links between business firms with complementary interests. Considering the dynamic changes in business requirements during the past decade, the need for close bank cooperation requires that branch banking fill a very definite service need. The bank has striven to meet this need for branches near businesses and retail customers throughout the service area.

BANK'S SOCIAL OBLIGATIONS STOCKHOLDERS LETTER

LETTER J-18

A partial letter that addresses the new viewpoint in banking.

> There has been increased demand that corporations reconsider their position and meet their obligations to society. Also, banking institutions have an important responsibility to lend financial support to such economic and social changes.
>
> As a bank offering a full range of commercial banking services, the bank has far-reaching social influence, and of course, commensurate duties and obligations. We have been fortunate to receive the stable confidence of society by making available

the fullest capabilities of our bank's network of domestic and foreign offices, abundant financial resources, information services and manpower.

ECONOMIC REVIEW STOCKHOLDERS LETTER

LETTER J-19

A partial letter that provides enlightening information on the world economy.

Last year saw no appreciable improvement in the world economy. According to the Organization for Economic Cooperation and Development, the growth rate for member nations averaged minus 0.1% two years ago, and dropped to minus 2% last year.

While on balance, the world economy showed improvement in price stability and balance of payments for last year, the inflation problem remained unsolved. Price trends for this year should not be viewed with extra enthusiasm, considering the prospects of a gradual expansion in the world economy. The employment situation, with rising unemployment rates, led policy makers to shift emphasis from fighting inflation to stabilizing the business cycle. This resulted in a relaxed monetary policy with a decline in interest rates.

CORPORATE BANKING—STOCKHOLDERS LETTER

LETTER J-20

A partial stockholders letter stating positive attributes of corporate banking functions.

In addition to strengthening traditional lending activities, the Bank expanded and diversified its financial services offered to the business community. The Bank has expanded and structured its facilities to successfully meet the needs of corporate customers.

The Bank has a variety of subsidiaries and affiliates in related areas—leasing, management consultation for small firms, entrusted computer services, venture capital—and together with consolidation of peripheral business lines to match its operational diversification, the Bank expects to meet more fully the needs of business customers.

INVESTMENT AND TRUSTEE BANKING
STOCKHOLDERS LETTER

LETTER J-21

A partial letter to inform the stockholder of the activities of an investment and trustee nature undertaken by the bank.

Last year, we saw large government bond issues offered. Under the bank's public investment policy, we were very active in this area. Also, sizable gains were posted in our stock investments as compared to the previous year, because of the new share allocations by solid corporations such as steel firms and electric power companies.

Annual increases in the amount of corporate bond issues for which the bank acts as trustee has held steady growth. In public offerings of straight corporate bonds, the Bank acted as representative trustee for 17 corporations and as co-trustee for 23 corporations.

These investment and trustee activities illustrate the integrated and overall financial facilities which the bank makes available to our business customers in addition to normal lending activities.

EMPLOYEE STOCK OWNERSHIP VALUE
TO STOCKHOLDER LETTER

LETTER J-22

A partial letter that assures other stockholders that their investment interest is compatible with the banker's success plans.

As Chairman of the Board of ABC Bank and the largest stockholder, I know that the most important motivational success plan for the bank results from entering into a partnership with our employees. History demonstrates that free enterprise is successful when the majority of staff members responsible for an organization are owners. You will see throughout our stockholders report, the importance of our partnership with staff members of the ABC Bank.

LIQUIDITY AND CAPITAL STRENGTH STOCKHOLDER LETTER

LETTER J-23

A partial letter that stresses an important factor of banking—liquidity and capital strength.

The capital strength of the bank and the surplus amounts of liquidity in the American economy presented the opportunity to add excellent marketable assets during the past year. Many of our corporate customers are leaders in their markets, which adds to the quality of the bank's loan portfolio. This quality has been reflected in the bank's loan loss experience which is quite favorable, considering the adverse impact on the banking industry from the weakened economic conditions.

FOREIGN EXCHANGE CURRENCY STOCKHOLDER LETTER

LETTER J-24

A partial letter that discusses foreign currency relationships to the American dollar.

The bank must respond to the adverse effects on earnings when a foreign currency is weakened against the American dollar. In a country where the debt is high in relation to assets, a *strengthening* of that country's currency against the dollar generally has an adverse effect on reported earnings. The debt is translated at the new, higher rate of exchange, and assumes a greater liability in American dollars. The bank looks forward to greater economic stability in the rates of exchange. Our larger corporate customers have operations in several foreign countries, which requires us to provide the optimum in foreign exchange services.

PRE-TAX EARNINGS STOCKHOLDER LETTER

LETTER J-25

A partial letter that highlights banking strength.

The pre-tax earnings of the Bank increased 31% to $4.2 million. Total deposits increased 7½%, while total bank assets rose 6%. During 19____, the Bank's cost of money was reduced. The combination of deposit growth, in addition to good loan demand and lower money costs, allowed the bank to increase earnings.

BANKING LOAN LOSSES STOCKHOLDERS LETTER

LETTER J-26

A partial letter to explain a critical banking risk—uncollectible loans.

ABC Bank's loss on uncollectible loans continues to decline as a percent of our loans outstanding. Our loan loss expense continues to be favorable at one-half of one percent, in line with our last five year loss expense average. These results are excellent since the ABC Bank has over 38% of the loan portfolio in consumer installment loans. The banking industry normally reports higher losses on installment consumer loans than on commercial loans.

MANAGING PENSION PLAN FUNDS STOCKHOLDERS LETTER

LETTER J-27

A partial letter that relates the banking value in trust handling of pension funds.

The ABC Bank's favorable record in managing pension plan funds within our Trust Department not only attracted a large volume of new pension fund accounts, but also resulted in substantial additional demand deposits from existing group pension accounts. Our marketing program resulted in a 45% increase from the previous year in this one segment of our trust business.

EQUAL OPPORTUNITY GOALS STOCKHOLDERS LETTER

LETTER J-28

A partial letter that informs the stockholders about the bank's progressive policy.

The ABC Bank believes in the nationwide goals of better representation of minority individuals and women at all job levels. Our staff is composed of 22% minority employees working in all departments, including bank officers. Women hold 42% of our banking positions—both managerial and clerical. Through training programs, our staff members are able to advance their careers with the bank regardless of sex, religion, race or creed. We are striving to provide a better tomorrow for all our staff members.

RETAIL BANKING SERVICES STOCKHOLDER LETTER

LETTER J-29

A partial letter that informs of new innovations in retail banking services.

Keeping abreast of the growing demand for retail banking services, the ABC Bank opened three new full-service branches during the past year. The bank also introduced two innovative services at all branches. The ABC DEBIT CASH CARD that permits customers to deposit or withdraw their own cash 24 hours a day. The customer express service line has been installed at most branches in order to assign entering customers from a master line to the first available teller. The express service has reduced the average waiting time for the bank's customers.

GROUP *K* LETTERS

The Ten Special Purpose
Purchasing Letters Needed
in Banking

Every bank officer at one time or another must initiate a purchase for the bank. In this group of letters, special purpose purchasing responses are compiled for the more difficult situations.

An important letter that should regularly be used by all banks is Letter K-1, which will eliminate the embarrassment of deciding what to do about gifts from a supplier.

Major letters are included to save time in requesting a price quotation; refusing to purchase, with appreciation extended to the supplier; and persuading a supplier to accept the return of defective products.

Purchasing letters must be carefully planned because suppliers offer better service to preferred customers. That status is important for the bank to maintain.

"NO GIFTS, PLEASE!" LETTER
LETTER K-1

Eliminate the conflict of interest problem by issuing a standard letter to suppliers about gifts and gratuities.

Gentlemen:

As the end of the current year approaches, we at ABC Bank would like to take this opportunity to express our appreciation to our suppliers for the excellent cooperation and support we have received during 19____.

We ask your help in maintaining the high ethical standard demand of ABC personnel. Therefore, please avoid embarrassment by refraining from offering any gifts or gratuities to any ABC Bank employee. The acceptance of gratuities is forbidden by bank policy. Your thoughts in this area are sincerely appreciated, but instead you will find our staff desires that you maintain your high level of service.

We wish you a bright and successful New Year.

Very truly yours,

REPLY TO A DROP IN PURCHASING LETTER

LETTER K-2

A bank is in a unique position in the purchase of any product. The company and the sales agent may be bank customers—as may any company supplying similar products. When asked why purchases are reduced or stopped, the answer must be sensitive to the bank's unique position.

Dear Supplier:

I cannot give a particular reason for our not buying as much as the previous year. Our needs are constantly changing as are our buying requirements.

The service you give the bank and the quality of the products have been satisfactory. Also, we have high regard for Mr. _____, your sales representative. I have found his services and suggestions to be of value to the bank.

Certainly, when we have further requirements that we feel your company can supply, be assured Mr. _____ will be consulted.

Sincerely,

SPECIAL THANKS TO A SUPPLIER LETTER

LETTER K-3

A letter of thanks is in order when a supplier performs service of significance to the bank. The next call for service will be promptly handled—even if another customer must wait.

Gentlemen:

I felt I should take this opportunity to express my appreciation for the excellent service support we received from your repair representatives during the past month. We had high expectations when the banking equipment was installed, and you have surpassed them. The strict standards and deadlines have been met by the new equipment.

Of course, equipment breakdowns are never anticipated, but I was particularly impressed with the prompt attention to our crisis when the system malfunctioned. I was also impressed with the breadth and depth of knowledge your firm has of the banking industry.

Last month, when our system went down, we were not out of operation for more than three hours. This is commendable. As far as I am concerned, continuing service is the real test of any equipment supplier, particularly in our remote location. I appreciate your concern for us.

Sincerely,

REQUEST FOR PRICE QUOTATION LETTER

LETTER K-4

A good business practice is to get several quotations for large purchases.

Dear Supplier:

As a customary practice, the ABC Bank requests price quotations for large purchases.

Therefore, we would appreciate receiving a quotation for the following items:

> *Quantity:*
>
> *Item:*

Please state in your price quotation whether freight is paid to destination or f.o.b. shipping point.

We require delivery on or before (*date*).

Thank you for your prompt handling of our purchase requests.

Cordially,

REFUSING TO PURCHASE A MAJOR ITEM LETTER

LETTER K-5

Inform the salesman and his company about your final decision and show appreciation for his assistance.

Dear Mr. —————:

The bank operations committee appreciated your extensive presentation of your equipment. The benefits of the purchase as proposed were convincing and thorough.

However, the committee felt the purchase must be deferred because of cost and operational change-overs that would be poorly timed with the opening of a new branch planned for the fall.

Again, we appreciate your time and efforts on our behalf.

Sincerely,

REQUEST FOR PRICING LETTER

LETTER K-6

The proper request for pricing will eliminate wasted time and correspondence in getting additional prices and material later.

Dear Sir:

After review of your sales material, we are interested in receiving a sample of computer forms that we can test on our equipment.

If the sample is suitable to our data processing staff, we will need prices on the enclosed form layout for continuous run. Please quote prices on 10,000 forms, 25,000 forms and 50,000 forms. We prefer the bank statement forms to be continuous in sets of 2,000, minimum.

Yours very truly,

QUESTIONING THE INVOICE LETTER

LETTER K-7

In checking invoices, occasionally the amounts do not agree with the purchase order or the quotes submitted to the bank.

Dear _____:

We have just reviewed your invoice number 21212 dated March 4, 19___, for the 5th Street Branch of the ABC Bank.

Since there appears to be a difference between the invoice and the purchase order price of the second item, we are holding the invoice until you have a chance to review your pricing. If you agree that the second item is billed incorrectly, we would appreciate a corrected invoice prior to our remitting payment.

Your prompt reply will be appreciated.

Cordially,

GETTING A FREE TRIAL OFFER LETTER

LETTER K-8

A quick letter to respond to a sales plan for more information and a trial offer.

Dear Sir:

I have just read your brochure regarding the savings available to the branches of our bank by using your _____ product.

The concept and information are interesting, but I cannot be sure if your _____ product is superior to the ones now in use at the branches. Since your proposal would result in a large investment by the bank, I am sure you would be willing to send us several samples for test purposes.

If your _____ product fulfills the promise in your marketing brochure, we will be able to use it.

I will be looking forward to receiving quantity prices and several samples.

Best regards,

ABC Bank

PUSHING THE RETURN OF DEFECTIVE PRODUCTS LETTER

LETTER K-9

When the quality is not suitable, a sales presentation is sometimes required to get the vendor to accept return of the product.

Dear _____:

We were disappointed in the latest shipment of installment loan forms. This shipment is not printed in the usual high excellence that we are accustomed to receiving from your company.

I have asked the Accounts Payable people to hold the invoice covering this shipment of 50,000 loan forms. As you know, we set very high standards for material that our bank customers receive. Perhaps it would be simpler for you to send a replacement shipment for order number 16278 covered by your invoice number 32221. Upon your written authorization, we will destroy the shipment on hand or return them freight collect to your plant.

We are due for a second shipment of 50,000 the first of next month on our order number 17344. Please re-check these forms prior to shipping, as we were greatly inconvenienced by the dispersal of the bad forms to all 16 branches of the bank before the quality error was discovered.

Please advise me as to your requirements for replacing the defective shipment at your earliest convenience.

Cordially,

"DON'T YOU WANT US TO BUY?" LETTER

LETTER K-10

When information about a proposed purchase has not been received on time, a follow-up letter should be sent.

Dear _____:

Perhaps there has been a misrouting of my letter of January 10, 19___ at your office. Usually you are very prompt in replying to purchase request information that we need at the ABC Bank in order to get purchase approval.

As quickly as possible, would you send me the price and delivery on 10,000 continuous run bank statement forms, special stock number 345k2?

Our present supply is running low and we need to place an order this week if your terms are acceptable to the bank. I look forward to your early response.

Sincerely,

GROUP *L* LETTERS

Ten Governmental Agency Letters

In this group of governmental agency letters, selected problem responses are presented.

The transfer of funds with the automated payments exchange (APEX) system is explained as vital to the future of banking. The benefits of APEX are many-fold. This letter has excellent reader benefit appeal. By selecting key paragraphs from the APEX letter, the bank can quickly use the material with other important groups.

With governmental agencies, the message must be stated early in the letter with a strong attention sentence. Long correspondence may not be acted upon for quite some time. It is just the nature of humans in receiving volumes of letters that the easiest request be handled first.

INTERNAL REVENUE SERVICE DISPUTE LETTER

LETTER L-1

Clearing up I.R.S. disagreements requires specific information, as this letter provided for a bank.

Department of the Treasury
Internal Revenue Service Center

Re: Federal Employer's Quarterly Tax Return
      December 31, 19____

Dear Sirs:

Enclosed is a copy, front and back, of our December 31, 19____ Form 941 which you claim has a balance due of $116.36. However, we have checked and re-checked our calculations and fail to see any error in the bank's report.

Please examine the enclosed data and then contact us as to your findings. If we are indeed in error, please notify us as to the specific correction required so we can make the necessary corrections and payment.

Sincerely,

PROBLEM TO COUNTY RECORDER LETTER

LETTER L-2

Recorder
County Courthouse

Enclosed is a copy of the General Warranty Deed pertaining to the purchase of land by the State Highway Department.

There is some concern by Mr. _____, the seller, that an adjustment in the tax record has not been completed. As you will note, the land sold to the Highway Department reduces the present acreage on which the bank holds a mortgage.

We would like verification that this land has been removed from Mr. _____ tax record. Your assistance is appreciated.

Cordially,

PARTICIPATION LOAN VERIFICATION BANK EXAMINER LETTER

LETTER L-3

Dear Examiner-in-charge:

This is to certify that the ABC Bank has a participation loan on the XYZ Company from the DEF Bank, with a balance of $25,000 which is due December 7, 19____.

Sincerely yours,

PAYMENT OF INTEREST ON CONSUMER DEMAND ACCOUNTS LETTER

LETTER L-4

A letter to legislators informing them of banking problems and requesting a response on their position.

Dear Congressman:

The members of the State Bankers Association reviewed in depth the Senate bills pending before Congress pertaining to the payment of interest on individual consumer accounts. It was expressed that bankers could stop this trend in the banking industry only for a short period of time, but could not stop it in the other financial institutions such as savings and loan, savings banks and credit unions.

Senate Bill No. 1668, introduced by the American Bankers Association was discussed and endorsed by the State Association in its present form.

The American Bankers Association bill limits the payment of interest to consumer demand accounts, requires that all financial institutions be allowed to have the same interest ceiling rates, provides that interest be paid on reserve balances at the Federal Reserve Banks and that financial institutions keep the same reserves on interest-bearing demand accounts.

If this concept of payment of interest on demand consumer deposits becomes a reality and, for competitive reasons, banks offer this service, then banks must find ways and means to increase their earnings in order to offset the additional expense incurred.

Your views and comments on this vital banking issue are of interest to us. Please inform us of your present position.

Cordially,

AUTOMATED PAYMENTS EXCHANGE LETTER

LETTER L-5

A clarification of the APEX or Automated Payments Exchange.

Dear —————:

Your information concerning the APEX SYSTEM has been reviewed. We appreciate the opportunity to be able to originate automatic payroll deposits through the automated clearing house.

We need clarification of the operational techniques as we recognize the United States government has been one of the strongest of all boosters in urging a system of paperless entries. Please give us more details about the operational functions of the automated clearing house, and how the automated clearing house system is beneficial to the bank.

Upon receipt of your information, we will make a final decision on how our bank can best utilize the APEX SYSTEM. We look forward to your response.

Sincerely,

PROFIT OPPORTUNITIES WITH AUTOMATED PAYMENTS EXCHANGE LETTER

.LETTER L-6

A letter from the automated clearing house in response to Letter L-5.

Dear ABC Bank:

Most bankers realize that the profit race is usually won by those who are creative, aggressive and constantly looking ahead. Automated clearing is going to present profit opportunities that do not exist. One example is the automated payroll deposits. This means, of course, that banks have an entirely new service to offer their corporate customers.

Smaller banks should receive a greater benefit from Automated Payment Exchange (APEX) than do larger banks in the initial years. Under our rules, the transfer of funds is made in good money on payday. Assume that the employer-company does its banking with a large urban bank and the employee with a suburban bank. Under the present paper check system, a suburban bank does not receive funds until the paycheck is endorsed, cashed, deposited and *cleared*. The time period can be two or three days or more. Under the APEX system, the suburban bank receives the money on payday in good funds.

There are two principal reasons for the automated clearing house and APEX system. First, the processing of paper checks should double in the next decade which will add more people and costs to the processing problem. Second, a paperless transfer of funds will save a lot of trees from being consumed for paper products. It takes a lot of trees to make enough paper to equal the 30 billion checks that are expected to be written this year.

Operationally, the automated clearing house works similar to the present check system; except we eliminate the flow of paper. The new system will provide electronic signals to replace the paper checks. The Automated Clearing House serves as a central place for gathering, sorting and dispatching the electronic signals.

We feel the APEX System has much to offer banks, companies

and employees. You have the opportunity to offer one of the newest banking benefits to your customers. Should you need further information, please contact us.

Cordially,

FEDERAL RESERVE MEMBERSHIP LETTER

LETTER L-7

A partial, unique letter concerning membership in the Federal Reserve.

The decline in the number of member banks raises concern about the continued ability of the Federal Reserve to regulate the supply of money and credit with reasonable precision, and about the ability of the System to employ varying levels of reserve requirements as a monetary policy tool.

Member banks are required to carry substantial reserves with the system in the form of non-earning assets. As a result, member banks have a "bottom line" disadvantage as compared with non-member banks, which are permitted to hold a high proportion of their required reserves in a form that yields direct or implicit return. Federal Reserve member banks presently bear an earnings burden not shared by non-member institutions of similar size.

BANK EXAMINER LETTER

LETTER L-8

A response to a recent bank examination.

Dear _____:

We have reviewed your recent examination report for the bank and appreciate the suggestions that you have made.

The items that you have taken exception to have been adjusted or corrected in accordance with your comments.

Enclosed is a summary of specific correction action taken in regards to our loan portfolio. We believe our items are now in accordance with your report

Cordially,

VETERANS ADMINISTRATION DEFAULT LETTER

LETTER L-9

A notice sent to the V.A. in compliance with the insurance requirements on a V.A. loan.

Veterans Administration:

Re: V.A. Loan File Number:

Dear _____:

The following bank loan guaranteed by the Veterans Administration is now in default:

Name of Borrower

Property Address

Balance Due

This loan is now three months in arrears. The Veteran has been
advised that the property is subject to foreclosure unless the
loan can be brought current.

We wish to advise you of the pending action in accordance with
your policy.

Yours truly,

COUNTY RECORDER DEED VERIFICATION LETTER

LETTER L-10

A letter sent to a distant county for verification of deed on record.

County Recorder

Dear _____:

Enclosed is a summary of the property deed for the estate of
the late Mr. _____.

Would you please verify that this information is correct according to your public records? Also, if possible, we would appreciate receiving a copy of the deed, certified as a true and
correct copy from your office. This information is needed for the
ABC Bank to complete the estate matters. The appropriate fees
are enclosed, made payable to your office.

Your assistance in promptly transmitting this information to us
will be greatly appreciated.

Cordially,

GROUP *M* LETTERS

Six Unusual Letters for Purchasing a Bank, Bank Mergers, and Incorporation

In the Group M letters, we have compiled six special and unusual letters. If you want to buy a bank, plan a bank merger or incorporate a bank holding company, you will find unique forms and letters in this group that have been used successfully by other bankers.

If you dream of owning your own bank someday, Letter M-1 offers the formula that one individual actually used to achieve his dream. His banking background was limited, but his financial ability was outstanding. The formula in Letter M-1 can be duplicated by others who want to buy a bank. You will notice how the request to borrow heavily for the purchase is delicately buried in the body of the letter. The proposal was sound and the loan was approved. The American Dream came true for another banker.

This group also deals with bank mergers, appointment of bank officers, bank proxy, incorporation voting ballot, and the resolution of the bank's board of directors to form a bank holding company.

"BUY YOUR OWN BANK" LETTER

LETTER M-1

This letter established a formal plan to purchase 80 percent of outstanding shares of state bank that was accepted.

Dear _____:

This is in answer to your request that I submit my plan to amortize the proposed debt which would be incurred to purchase 80% of the outstanding shares of the ABC State Bank.

My plan as outlined herein, is predicated upon the assumption that the purchase of the stock will be accomplished in accordance with the Sales Agreement as prepared by _____, of which you have a copy, I believe.

According to this agreement, it will require funds in the amount of $401,749 in 19___ to be paid to the stockholders, which is itemized as follows:

Payment to be made upon execution of the Sales Agreement	$ 10,000
Payment to be made to majority stockholders at closing date, November 1, 19___	224,150
Funds required to purchase 192 shares from minority stockholders at an amount not to exceed 1.25 of Book Value (872.91)	167,599
	$401,749

I propose to pay the above amount as follows:

Issue a personal check for the initial payment	$ 10,000
Pay with proceeds from the sale of _____ Bank (Estimated after deducting Capital Gains Taxes and the amount owed to Bank of XYZ ($67,000.00)	211,000
Pay with proceeds from sale of stock (estimated after taxes)	15,000
Obtain loan for the balance from XYZ Bank	117,749
	$343,749

The total purchase price for 960 shares of the _____ Bank is itemized as follows:

768 shares from Major Stockholder	$806,400
192 shares from Minority stockholders	167,599
	$973,999

Total purchase price forwarded	$973,999
Deduct payments made in 19___	343,749
Balance to be paid in 19___ and 19___	$630,250

This balance of $630,250 will require a loan in that amount from the _____ Bank of XYZ, which added to the $117,749 previously itemized would make the total loan $689,999.

The CPA firm has, as you know, run a cash flow projection which indicates that the debt to purchase the State Bank amortizes in 12 years, using the following assumptions:

Beginning assets	$9,200,000.00
Beginning capital	806,000.00
Annual growth	5%
Capital Assets % of retention	7.5%
Annual earnings—% of assets	1.06%
Average interest rate	8.0%
Organization Cost	$10,000.00
Insurance	.00

I talked with a CPA this morning and he promised to deliver to you a copy of the cash flow projection and to send one to me, as quickly as he can get printouts from the computer.

I hope this information will enable you to get approval from your loan committee on my loan application soon, so we can present the Sales Agreement to the Stockholders.

Sincerely,

ANNOUNCEMENT OF BANK MERGER LETTER

LETTER M-2

A special letter to key commercial bank clients and potential clients.

Effective on January 10, 19___, the DEF Bank will be a part of the ABC Bank and Trust Company. This merger gives added strength to the new combined ABC Bank and Trust Company.

The staff of the DEF Bank will remain to serve you through the added resources of the combined banking organization, with increased reserves and operational skill. Now our minimum loan, based on our reserve strength, increases from $80,000 to one million dollars for a single banking customer.

I'm sure you will be pleased that your old friends at DEF Bank will remain to serve you with new and better banking benefits. We will strive to retain your banking loyalty.

Cordially,

INCORPORATION VOTING BALLOT FORM

LETTER M-3

While no particular ballot form is generally required, the form used here is for one vote per share.

THE ABC BANK & TRUST COMPANY
ANNUAL MEETING (*DATE*), 19___

I, the undersigned, do hereby vote _____ shares of stock for the following individuals to serve as directors for the ensuing year:

_____

_____

_____

_____

_____

(Stockholder signs here)

By *(Or signature of holder of proxies)*
Proxy

APPOINTMENT OF BANK OFFICERS FORM LETTER

LETTER M-4

Instrument of Appointment of Officers
of
the ABC Bank

The ABC Bank hereby appoints the following persons as officers of the bank to hold the offices set opposite their respective names subject to removal at any time, with or without cause, by the ABC Bank.

Pursuant to the General Loan and Investment Regulations, the following lending authorities are effective immediately:

NAME   OFFICE   LENDING AUTHORITY LIMIT

THE   ABC   BANK

By

PROXY FROM THE BANK LETTER

LETTER M-5

KNOW ALL MEN BY THESE PRESENTS, that the ABC Bank, a Corporation, owning and holding _____ shares of common stock of the XYZ Corporation, does appoint _____ as its true and lawful attorney to attend the annual meeting of the stockholders of the XYZ Corporation on _____, 19___; and to vote for the Bank and in its name as its proxy and representative of the number of votes which the Bank would be entitled to cast.

IN WITNESS WHEREOF, said Corporation has hereunto caused its name and seal to be affixed as duly authorized by its Board of Directors by resolution duly passed and adopted on the _____ day of _____ 19___.

ABC BANK & TRUST COMPANY

                                            (Seal)

By_____President

By_____Secretary

RESOLUTION OF BOARD OF DIRECTORS TO FORM BANK HOLDING COMPANY

LETTER M-6

Resolution sent to the Board of Governors of the Federal Reserve System as part of the application to become a bank holding company.

RESOLUTION

Applicant's Board of Directors, or other appropriate governing body, shall authorize the execution and delivery of this application to the Board by a resolution substantially in the form as that which follows (in lieu thereof, a brief description of the proposal along with a copy of the continuing resolution authorizing it, may be furnished):

RESOLVED, that _____, the _____
            (Name)   *(Title of Officer)*
and _____, the _____
            (Name)   *(Title of Officer)*

_____
(Name of Applicant)

(hereinafter referred to as Applicant), or either of them, be, and they hereby are, authorized and empowered for and in the name and on behalf of Applicant to execute and deliver to the Board of Governors of the Federal Reserve System, pursuant to section 4(c)(8) of the Bank Holding Company Act of 1956, as amended, an application for approval by the Board of the acquisition or retention of (brief description of proposal including the name and address of any company involved):

_____
_____
_____
_____
(Name of Company)

_____
(Address)

CERTIFICATE

I Hereby Certify that the foregoing is a true and correct copy of a resolution adopted by the _____
                              (Governing Body)
of_____ at a meeting duly called and held at
_____ on the _____ day of _____.
19_____, at which meeting a quorum was presented and voted.

_____
                              Secretary

GROUP *N* LETTERS

Eight Firing-line Internal Bank Operations Memos

Internal bank operations memos as included in this letter group become the backbone of banking policy. To be sure, memos are certain to be read. These special communicators receive reading priority from a busy bank staff.

For clarity of message, it is preferable to communicate in writing. In a memo, it is preferable to identify the subject on a separate subject line. A sentence or two should explain the problem followed by the details, benefits or analysis. If recommendations are incorporated in a memo, alert readers will instinctively know they can skip to the last unit or paragraph in long memos for knowledge of the recommendations.

The memos in this group provide the bank with useful memos to define authority, improve banking services, present bad news to the staff and establish banking policy.

AUTHORITY OF BANK PRESIDENT MEMO
LETTER N-1

Innovative Internal Bank Memo for Operations to establish special chain-of-command authority.

Memorandum

Subject: *AUTHORITIES RESERVED TO THE BANK PRESIDENT.*

To: ALL BANK OFFICERS.

To avoid misunderstanding concerning policy matters which are required to be submitted to the President for review and approval prior to any binding commitments, or change of policy; it is important that all bank officers review the following areas, paying particular attention as to how each respective responsibility is affected.

Items requiring final approval by the President are:

PRODUCTS AND SERVICES

1. Significant changes in the general pricing pattern of interest rates, discounts and service charges.
2. Acquisitions of new activities or companies, and the reduction or elimination of existing activities or services.
3. Significant changes in billing procedures, customers relations policy, credit criteria and collection policy.

INTERNAL CONTROLS

1. Final approval of operating plans and budgets and any substantial revisions thereof.
2. Major changes in form or content of management reports submitted to Senior Management or the President.
3. Purchase or investments in excess of $25,000.

ORGANIZATION AND STAFF

1. Changes in organization, concept or method, or reassignment in duties at the rank of Second Vice-President and above.
2. General adjustments in salary scales and employee benefits. Changes in policy affecting employee relationships.
3. Statements to the press or public stating company policy.

Approved:

The President

CONSUMER CREDIT PACKAGE MEMO

LETTER N-2

To: All branch bank officers

Subject: Consumer Credit Services

We want to make your customers aware of the variety of the bank's consumer credit services. Each program is designed to meet different, but overlapping consumer credit needs. Proper and profitable marketing of these services entails skillful interviewing and the ability to offer the service best suited to the borrower's needs and circumstances.

Every credit request presents a variety of marketing opportunities:

Large amounts—$500 to $5,000—for autos, home improvements, etc.

- Installment Loans
- Emphasizing advantages of single statement accounts
- Opportunity to sell regular and special checking accounts
- Overdraft banking credit

Moderate amounts—under $1,000—short terms less than a year, unexpected bills, indefinite amounts:

- Overdraft banking for checking account customer
- If not a depositor—suggest checking *and* overdraft banking
- Bank credit card

Small amounts up to $300 for shopping, weekend cash needs:

- Ideal for bank credit card
- Bank credit card cash advance
- *AND* a checking account for convenient payment of the bank credit card's one monthly billing.

It sounds like a lot of service—and it is! Service is the most important item we can offer the customer.

Yet the best aspect of service is—SPEED. Between branch approvals and phone applications, virtually every deserving customer can receive credit in a matter of hours—even minutes. The introduction of a checking account and credit services will create a solid benefit to your customer for years to come.

TELL THE BANK STORY MEMO

LETTER N-3

Dear Staff:

Every day, hundreds of new folks move into our community and are potential savings and loan customers of ABC Bank. They just need to be told about the services we offer.

New residents are often hesitant to apply for installment loans because they have no established credit record in the city, and do not know the ease of applying for an ABC Bank loan. So when you provide a loan application or savings introduction card with a warm invitation to use our services, you do our customers a favor, the bank a favor and *yourself* a favor.

Each savings account opened or installment loan approved earns you points in the ABC Bank staffer contest. Top prize is a $500 savings account for you. Ten prizes in all.

Helping new customers is another must service of ABC Bank. *But*, right now it earns prize points for you. Each application and savings introduction card has your personal identification number on it so you will receive credit for the new business. We hope you will do your best.

President

P.S. Good luck on that $500 top prize.

BAD NEWS MEMO RELATING COFFEE PRICES TO THE PRIME RATE

LETTER N-4

Bad news to the bank staff can be softened by relating to familiar items. Plan to reduce employee complaints.

To: Bank Staff
Subject: Coffee prices and the prime rate.

The ABC Bank's cafeteria will provide FREE COFFEE to everyone in the cafeteria from 10 A.M. to 2 P.M. on July 25,

19____. Won't you join us in this last gesture of farewell to the 20¢ cup of coffee?

The cafeteria service organization is forced to raise prices on a number of items in the cafeteria, including the raise to 25¢ for a cup of coffee. Rising prices beyond our control has forced the price increase. The cafeteria service organization has no better control over food prices than we at ABC Bank have over the fluctuations in the prime rate. We country banks have that problem.

Still, we find by our survey that the bank cafeteria is more gentle on the pocketbook than outside restaurants.

POLICY AND PROCEDURE FOR MAIL-IN LOAN REQUESTS MEMO

LETTER N-5

A partial operational memo for policy control of the banking loan function.

PURPOSE

To set forth the procedures to be followed by the various departments participating in the handling of credit card loan requests under the Mail-in Cash Advance Program.

INTRODUCTION

Through direct mail solicitation, all bank credit card accounts have been offered the opportunity to apply by mail for a cash advance loan. The initial campaign provided all cardholders in good standing, with an introductory cash advance request form. To make this opportunity continuously available to approved advance seekers, a regular request form is enclosed and mailed with the loan check.

The procedures set forth in the attached manual reflect the operations to be performed by the various personnel concerned with the mail-in cash advance program. The manual details the following important steps:

1. Control batch grouping of cash advance requests
2. The Credit Department authorization operation
3. Disposition of approved requests
4. Disposition of disapproved requests
5. Cashier's processing of approved requests
6. The data processing operation
7. Mailroom and microfilm operations

8. Return of undeliverable check

9. Error control processing

YOUR RESPONSIBILITY

You are requested to review the entire procedure in order to be familiar with the total operation. The sections that detail your specific responsibility must be studied carefully for your participation in an error-free operation.

SECURITIES AUTHORIZATION MEMO

LETTER N-6

A memo sent from a correspondent bank.

Subject: Securities Authorization

Please consider this authorization to charge the account of the ABC Bank upon delivery from XYZ Company, $30,000 at 5.25% City of AB Water and Electric Revenue Bonds; due 4/1/82.

The amount should be $31,494.60. Please retain the bonds for safekeeping and send us a receipt. Thank you.

Cordially,

Executive Vice-President

RESULTS OF EMPLOYEE SURVEY MEMO

LETTER N-7

Inform the staff of both the strengths and weaknesses in any employee survey undertaken.

ALL MEMBERS OF THE BANK STAFF

The results of the staff survey taken a few months ago have now been compiled. The study makes it clear in appraising your job and the bank that you feel there are both strengths and weaknesses in working at the ABC Bank.

On the positive side, a vast majority feel that banking is a pleasant career with friendly associates at ABC Bank. Employee morale is extremely high.

A Manpower Study Group has been initiated to explore the weaknesses that have been highlighted. The Group will evaluate steps that can be taken to build on our strengths and to improve weak areas. Three key factors will be reviewed:

1. Making it easier for you to bring problems to management's attention
2. Improving our training standards
3. Modifying our work scheduling

The improvements in these areas will be announced as constructive action; implemented in light of the results of the survey.

We want the ABC Bank to be an even better place for you to work.

President

60-MINUTE MEN AND WOMEN MORALE MEMO

LETTER N-8

A unique image-building morale memo.

Memo: To Bank Staff
From: The President

All of us are familiar with the "Minute Men" of the American Revolution. We of the banking industry must not only be "Minute Men and Minute Women," but also "60-Minute Men and Women." To attain a thorough understanding of the banking business in modern society, we must work every minute of every hour of every day.

It takes people with initiative and enthusiasm to do a job—informed people always do a better job. Your efforts reflect our image, and banks want to create a good one in the eyes of the public—our customers. Everything that you and I do, every contact that we make, creates an image in the eyes of our customers.

Do we—by our dress, our actions, our deportment—give a favorable impression to our customers? The image that we create with banking customers will do much to gain their banking volume and loyalty. For us—promotions, salary increases, more employee benefits and a larger share of the banking business.

If we can prepare to accept rigid standards of performance from ourselves, then we all will share in the better things that life has to offer.

President

Appendix

Quick Reference Salutation for Titled Addressee

Individual	Address	Salutation
Ambassador	The Honorable ———— United States Ambassador	Dear Mr. Ambassador:
Archbishop	The Most Reverend ————	Your Excellency: or Dear Archbishop ————:
Bishop	The Most Reverend Bishop ————	Your Excellency: or Dear Bishop ————:
Cabinet Member —U.S.	The Honorable ———— Secretary of Washington, D. C. 20520	Dear Mr. Secretary: or Dear Mr. ————:
Cardinal	His Eminence, ————	Your Eminence: or Dear Cardinal ————:
Chaplain	Captain ————, U.S.A.F. or Chaplain ————, U.S.A.F.	Dear Chaplain ————:
Chief Justice —U.S.	The Honorable ————, Chief Justice of the United States	Dear Mr. Chief Justice:
City Commissioner	The Honorable ————, City Commissioner of ————	Dear Mr. ————:

Congress-man	The Honorable ———, House of Representatives	Dear Congressman ———:
Dean— College	Dean ———, School of Business Administration	Dear Dean ———:
Governor	The Honorable ———, Governor of ———	Dear Governor ———:
Judge	The Honorable ———, Judge of Common Pleas Court	Dear Judge ———:
Mayor	The Honorable ———, Mayor of ———	Dear Mayor ———:
Minister	The Reverend ——— or Pastor ———	Dear Reverend ———: or Dear Pastor ———:
Pope	His Holiness	Most Holy Father:
President —U.S.	The Honorable ———, President of the United States	Dear Mr. President:
Priest	The Reverend ———	Dear Reverend Father:
Professor	Professor ———	Dear Mr. ———:
Rabbi	Rabbi ———	Dear Rabbi ———:
Senator— U.S.	The Honorable ———, United States Senate	Dear Senator ———:
Vice- President —U.S.	The Honorable ———, Vice-President of the United States	Dear Mr. Vice President:

INDEX